ABOUT THE PUBLISHER

New York Institute of Finance

... more than just books.

NYIF offers practical, applied training and education in a wide range of formats and topics:

* *Classroom training:* evenings, mornings, noon-hours
* *Seminars and conferences:* one-, two-, and three-day introductory, intermediate-, and professional-level programs
* *Customized training:* need-specific programs conducted on your site or ours; in New York City, throughout the United States, anywhere in the world
* *Independent study:* self-paced learning—basic, intermediate, or advanced
* *Exam preparation:* NASD licensing (including Series 3, 6, 7, 24, 27, 63); C.F.A.; state life and health insurance

Subjects of books and training programs include the following:

* Account Executive Training
* Brokerage Operations
* Currency Trading
* Futures Trading
* International Corporate Finance
* Investment Analysis

* Options Trading
* Securities Transfer
* Selling Securities
* Technical Analysis
* Treasury Management
* Yield Curve Analysis

When Wall Street professionals think **training***, they think NYIF.*

For further information, please call or write to us. Please specify your areas of interest—classroom training, custom programs, independent-study courses, exam preparation, or books—so that we can respond promptly to your inquiry.

New York Institute of Finance
70 Pine Street
New York, NY 10270–0003
212 / 344–2900
FAX: 212 / 514-8423
TELEX: 238790

Simon & Schuster, Inc.   A Gulf + Western Company
"Where Wall Street Goes to School" ™

SECURITIES ANALYSIS

SECURITIES ANALYSIS

A Personal Seminar

NEW YORK INSTITUTE OF FINANCE

Library of Congress Cataloging-in-Publication Data

Securities analysis.

Includes index.
1. Investment analysis.   2. Stocks.   3. Finance,
Personal.   I. New York Institute of Finance.
HG4529.S43   1989   332.63'2   88-34504
ISBN 0-13-658204-4

This publication is designed to provide accurate and authoritative
information in regard to the subject matter covered. It is sold with the
understanding that the publisher is not engaged in rendering legal,
accounting, or other professional service. If legal advice or other
expert assistance is required, the services of a competent professional
person should be sought.

*From a Declaration of Principals Jointly Adopted by a Committee
of the American Bar Association and a Committee of Publishers
and Associations*

New York Institute of Finance
(NYIF Corp.)
70 Pine Street
New York, NY 10270-0003

Contents

3. Market Views   37

4. Reading Financial Statements   71

Bull markets allow you to make investment mistakes now and then. You can place your money in almost any stock and not get hurt—and perhaps do quite well.

In uncertain times, however, you need to pick your investments very carefully. Essential to profitable investments is securities analysis—the body of knowledge and techniques that enable investors to pick the right stocks for their individual investment objectives.

This easy-to-use, self-teaching guide is designed to show you how to evaluate stocks in light of your personal investment goals or limitations. It explains the basic elements of securities analysis and discusses, in a practical way, methods to use for deciding on the purchase of specific stocks. You will learn:

- The different types of common stocks.
- How to assess investment risk.
- How to analyze particular stocks, industry groups, and the economy as a whole.
- What you need to know to read financial statements.

As part of the hands-on format, illustrative situations challenge you to respond to specific situations, thereby developing your ability and confidence in analysis and decision making.

All you need, besides this Personal Seminar, is a pocket calculator—and the desire to improve the returns on your equity investments.

1
The Individual Investor

Risk Aversion Versus Risk Taking

Which Type of Investor Are You?

Before you define your investment game plan, you must understand which type of investor you are (or want to be). Once you define your game plan, you must stick to the three C's of the intelligent investor: (1) cover, (2) courage, and (3) contingency.

To determine which type of investor you are, you may need to compile a short history of your investment patterns. If personal savings or certificates of deposit (CDs) have been your only investment, then, depending on the type of cash investment and the time period over which you made the investment, you have earned 5 percent to 8 percent returns. Money market funds are a very secure investment, but "freezing" your cash in CDs with fixed yields may not be the best way to maximize your return.

Accepting risk is a *fundamental* aspect of investing money. Understanding the historical patterns of the return on your investment requires the homework that most of us are either unable or unwilling to do. This book is a guide for security investment. It provides readers with a guide to decision making and helps them make the decisions that they may have hired professional investors to make for them. It also enables readers to make informed decisions when their investment advisers ask them if they are willing to "up the ante" on their current risk for higher expected yields.

It is important to understand the role expectations and risk play in formulating an investment strategy. All investors would prefer to earn high returns on their investments and take no risk. Unfortunately, investments do not work in this manner. When you invest your money in investments that do not have guaranteed returns, you *expect* to earn a return with magnitude, but this return is *not earned for certain*. This uncertainty is called the riskiness of the investment.

Investors are said to be risk adverse (risk averters). When choosing among investments with equal expected returns, a risk averter will invest in the investment with the least risk. A risk averter, however, will not necessarily invest in the investment with the least risk if the alternative investments have a higher expected rate of return. The choice will depend on the individual investor because different risk averters may have different risk preferences. Thus, two dimensions of an investment must be considered in every investment strategy: its expected return and its riskiness. Each investor must choose the level of risk he or she is willing to accept and then must adopt the investment strategy that maximizes the expected return for that level of risk.

Investors choose different investment strategies for four reasons. First, alternative strategies may offer the same expected return and risk. Second, some strategies cannot be adopted by all investors because of institutional reasons (e.g., minimum amount of money that must be invested). Third, investors may not agree on the expected return or the riskiness of a particular investment. Finally, and perhaps most importantly, investors have different risk preferences. Commodity traders, investors concerned with inflation protection, newly married couples, middle-aged professionals, and retirees have different risk preferences. These differences are also evident in institutional investors. For example, insurance companies, mutual funds, and pension funds investors are characterized as either *adventurous* or *conservative* in their investments.

Studies have shown that even though individual investors are risk adverse, they tend to invest their wealth in only one or two stocks. Paradoxically, people who adopt this investment strategy accept greater than necessary risk for the expected return. Putting all your financial nest eggs in one or two baskets (investments) is an investment strategy with unnecessary risk because it *lacks* diversification.

Keep Your Alpha High and Your Beta Low

What does "Keep your alpha high and your beta low" mean? Alpha and beta, which are statistical measurements of the performance and riskiness of securities, respectively, are two of the key or cardinal concepts in securities analysis. As a fundamental strategy for people who want to have a "good" investment performance, it is imperative to understand how risk is measured and how beta and alpha are used. The so-called *beta* coefficient relates the volatility of a security to the volatility of the market as a *whole*. The *alpha* indicates whether a stock had a higher or lower rate of return than another stock with the *same* beta, or whether the stock performed better or worse against the market than its *beta alone would have predicted*. The "alpha factor," as it is called by professional investors, indicates *nonmarket* historic influences that are unique to each stock. Selecting a sufficient number of stocks with *positive* alphas, however, does not necessarily deliver a performance better than the betas alone would have predicted for market movement *as a whole;* the problem here is that alphas from historic data do not necessarily continue in the future. Furthermore, as you add more stocks to your portfolio, the *diversification* tends to decrease the chance of getting a *positive* alpha and actually increases the chance of a zero alpha. In fact, your portfolio's volatility becomes much like the *market* itself. Does this sound confusing? Actually, it's not. Inasmuch as theoretical frameworks attempt to capture the patterns of risk, they themselves have *measurable* confidence.

Beta Risk

Over the years, various stock indicators have experienced patterns of usage with some that were once in vogue falling out of fashion. Although the beta may not be in the spotlight as much as it used to be, many individual investors who are risk averters still rely on it. Here's how it works. If Computerex moves up three points each time the market gains 1 point, Computerex has a *beta* of three. The beta, or riskiness, of Computerex is *high* since a small fluctuation in the market (up or down) is associated with a large fluctuation in this stock. Electrix, a customer-owned hydroelectric plant, moves up 0.9 points each time the market gains one point. What is the Electrix beta? Right, it is 0.9. Is Electrix more or less stable than Computerex? Right again, it is *more* stable. When the market goes up,

TABLE 1.1

Stock	Beta	Alpha
AAR Corp.	0.83	0.40
AVX Corp.	2.27	−1.03
AITS, Inc.	−0.17	−3.25
AVM Corp.	0.50	1.77

SOURCE   *Standard & Poor's Stock Price Index.*

Electrix will go up too, but less rapidly than Computerex. Conversely, when the market goes down, Electrix will go down too, but not as much as Computerex.

From the standpoint of risk, if an investor wishes to take higher risks, he or she will buy stocks with high betas, since these stocks gain more sharply than the market and provide greater long-term profitability. Similarly, in the short run, these same stocks require extensive watching, since they can become high stakes losers when the market declines.

Take a look at the stocks in Table 1.1 and rank them from *highest* risk to *lowest* risk, based only on their *beta* values.

QUESTION

Place the stocks in order from *lowest* to *highest* relative beta.

ANSWER

AITS, Inc., AVM Corp., AAR Corp., AVX Corp.

QUESTION

Which stock has a beta *closest* to overall market performance?

ANSWER

AAR Corp.

Beta measures the co-movement of a firm's expected return with the expected return of the "market." Many issues must be addressed to estimate a firm's beta. For example, beta can be estimated statistically using historic stock returns. Even this simple estimation method raises many issues, however. These include the return interval (daily, weekly, monthly, and so on), the number of returns in the estimation period (1, 2, . . . , 10 or more years of data), and the type of statistical analysis (ordinary least squares regression analysis, random coefficients regression analysis, and so on). An alternative approach is to use other financial data such as income statements, balance sheets, lines of business, and the like to estimate beta statistically. Fortunately, investors do not have to estimate beta themselves because beta estimates are available commercially from investment and financial analysis firms.

Most studies indicate that high-beta corporations do much better in a rising market than low-beta firms. Naturally, the studies also indicate that these same firms do worse during a falling market. On the whole, though, high-beta stocks do *not* outperform low-beta stocks.

Although the theoretical derivation of beta is discussed in a later chapter, it is important to point out that beta is only one of several measures of risk that are used in securities analysis. Beta is derived under certain assumptions that do not hold in reality and, hence, is not the perfect risk measure. Other economic factors relevant to the riskiness of an investment are purchasing power risk, interest rates, business cycles, market risk, and exchange rate risks. These factors, which are interrelated with each other and with beta, are discussed in Chapter 2.

Investment Objectives

Portfolio management is a full-time business. There is no such thing as a part-time investment strategy. You must make your money *work* for you. We stress the importance of employing financial institutions to assist you when you cannot examine your investments on a *daily* basis. Most research indicates that *both* individual and institutional investors do not manage their portfolios effectively. They do not reevaluate the riskiness of their investments on a timely basis, nor do they recognize the consequences of poor investment performance. Modern portfolio management theory must be incorporated into *actual* investment practices in order to improve the return on invested dollars.

FIGURE 1.1

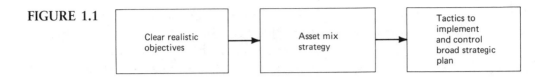

There are three critical elements to consider when formulating investment objectives:

1. Define the *objectives clearly* and *realistically.*
2. Determine an *asset-mix strategy* that will help achieve the investment objectives.
3. Adopt operating *tactics that will implement and control the broad strategic investment plan.*

Since capital market conditions change constantly, diligent and immediate adjustment to market trends is required in order to achieve financial goals in the long run. Few investors, however, have such diligence. They find it far easier to "wait out" the market shifts in the hope that recent losses will reverse themselves. This strategy is negligent and has irreversible effects on many portfolios. Let's examine the needs and constraints of various types of investors and review their investment behavior patterns. In the discussion we will try to differentiate between what investors *should* do and what they *actually* do.

For the Individual Investor, Cycle Staging and Risk Taking

Two important factors that influence the investment strategy of the individual investor are (1) the investor's stage in the life cycle and (2) his or her psychological makeup—the ability to withstand the stress and tensions of risk taking.

Life Cycles of Investors

The term *life cycle* encompasses three key stages in the life of the individual: young investor, individual at midstream, and individual near retirement.

Most analysts agree that because young investors are inexperienced, they should *not* take big risks without in-depth knowledge of the investment. Since time is the one thing youth has in abundance, young investors should place emergency monies in money market funds and invest their remaining assets in a portfolio that encourages growth for capital appreciation. Mutual funds are ideal for the young and inexperienced. Quality shares in these investments tend to increase as dividends and gains accumulate. Wealth accumulation via regular monthly savings and an investment program aimed at achieving long-term capital gains is the best strategy for young investors with an income of $40,000 and assets approximating $10,000. The investment portfolio may also include a tax-managed trust for tax-deferred compounding and growth. Excess cash flow can be used for monthly additions to mutual funds and tax-managed trusts.

At midstream the primary investment objectives of young couples change to overall reduction of current income taxes. Capital should be accumulated on a "tax-advantaged" basis. At the same time, maintenance of sufficient liquidity for purchases such as a new home is essential as families grow. Although business professionals coming into the prime of their careers may not yet have reached their peak salaries, they are usually experiencing greater financial security and mobility than at earlier stages of their lives. A joint income of $85,000 and assets of $80,000 could be allocated as follows (assuming federal and state taxes hover around $20,000 and yearly living expenses do not exceed $38,000):

Diversified stock portfolio or growth mutuals for capital appreciation	$30,000
Tax-managed trust for tax-deferred compounding and liquidity	20,000
Developmental limited partnership for reduction of current tax liability—offers a tax-advantaged cash flow position	10,000
Real estate limited partnership for capital appreciation and tax-sheltered income	10,000
Tax-deferred income via an IRA or 401(k) plan	4,000
Emergency cash held in money market checking account	6,000

Excess cash flow is used for monthly additions to the tax-managed trust and stock portfolios.

Many couples who do *not* enjoy good cash positioning have not planned for their children's college educations; consequently, at a time when capital growth is imperative for secured retirement, they must spend most of their income for the children's educations. The lesson is simple: plan for college expenses *from your child's birth*. About $10,000 to $15,000 must be invested at the birth of each child to ensure more than sufficient funds for college when the child reaches the age of 18. Parents who neglect this responsibility find themselves without the capital they need at this critical investment period. Plan now or pay later is one of the most valuable lessons one can learn from investment analysis.

Investors at midstream are financially more mature and sophisticated than young investors. Funds can be utilized more aggressively, and an entire gamut of investment opportunities may be considered. Discussions of cyclical stocks in later chapters will show how these investments (chosen at the appropriate stage of the business cycle) will pay big returns. At this stage, investors can buy on margin to enhance profitability, sell short, look into special situations, and consider convertible bonds or warrants. Switching from stocks to bonds to take advantage of interest rate trends (as well as tax-exempt state and municipal bonds) is a viable investment option during this period. Tax-sheltered investments, real estate, stock gifts to children, and even *commodities and financial futures* all provide attractive tax advantages.

Psychological Makeup of Investors

Psychological makeup refers to the investor's aversion to risk. The ability and desire to take risk vary greatly among people, but confidence in earning capacity encourages risk taking perhaps more than any other factor. Even though many young couples wish to preserve their painfully accumulated capital, they are confident they can replace losses and will aim at higher expected investment returns that go along with higher risks. Those who are content with low anticipated returns may find their portfolio growth remains stagnant at probably the *only* time in their lives they will be able to recover their losses.

Risk aversion peaks as couples reach their mid-50s and continues into their retirement years. Investors between the ages of 55 and 65 take fewer speculative chances in the pursuit of capital gains and high returns. They realize not much time remains in their lives to recover capital losses from speculative investments. At this point in life most investors shift their investments to fixed income benefits (i.e., Social Security and retirement funds). Their overall objective becomes the highest income consistent with safety, rather than speculative investments or *long*-term capital gains.

Let's examine a successful couple in their mid-50s. Assuming they are both professionals with a joint income of $175,000 and assets of $250,000, they will have approximately $70,000 to $80,000 in discretionary income and will pay between $48,000 and $58,000 in taxes. If the couple has $10,000 in a money market fund with checking account privileges (for emergencies), they could have an investment portfolio as follows:

Diversified high-quality common stocks (portfolio)	$50,000
Tax-managed trust for tax-deferred compounding and liquidity	30,000
Municipal bonds with staggered maturities (maximum 10 to 12 years)	100,000
Developmental limited partnerships for reduction of current tax liability and tax-advantaged cash flow	30,000
Real estate limited partnership for capital appreciation and tax-sheltered income	25,000
Tax-deferred income via an IRA or 401(k) plan	5,000
Emergency cash held in money market checking account	10,000

Overall, most investors maintain a middle-of-the-road attitude toward risk, and female investors tend to be more conservative than their male counterparts—possibly because they expect to live longer. Several studies have concluded that risk taking is *positively* related to income, but *negatively* related to age. This makes sense. The New

York Stock Exchange found that 69 percent of shareholders hold only one or two common stocks (49 percent of shareholders hold only one while 20 percent hold two). Is this surprising? You bet it is!

Number of Common Stocks	Percentage Held by All Adult Shareholders	
1	49%	69%
2	20	
3 to 7	22	
8 or more	9	
Total	100	
Base	753	

SOURCE   New York Stock Exchange, mid-1985.

?.91

Nine-one percent of *all* shareholders have fewer than eight separate stock issues in their portfolios. These portfolios are more risky than other types of investments the same individuals are willing to make. Ironically, when these investors were polled on portfolio diversification, most agreed it was a *good* idea. They obviously don't follow their own good advice on this issue.

Who Is the Average Investor?

The New York Stock Exchange recently completed a demographic study to answer the question, Who is the "average shareholder"? The study found the average investor fits the following profile:

	1985	Present
Age	44	34 (married female)
Household income	$37,000	$35,000
Median portfolio	$6,200	$2,200

Indicators suggest that investors are becoming younger, and that more married women are planning their financial futures than ever before. Women may truly be *liberating* themselves from the hardships of old age.

For the Institutional Investor, Obligations, Regulations, Taxation, and Intangibles

The institution's obligations to its clients, such as the preservation of pension funds, are critical to the institutional investor. Unlike the personal investor, institutions must adhere to certain legal regulations. The external investment environment and regulatory constraints (or considerations) govern institutional decision making. Intangibles such as the psychology of its clients or the mindset of an institution's *own* personnel contribute to the complex nature of the institutional investor. Even competitive practices among institutions themselves add to the stress of risk taking.

Each of these factors influences institutional investment objectives. In an attempt to balance often conflicting objectives, institutions must maintain their own marketability, liquidity, and firm control over capital gains—all this while ensuring the safety of their investments. Cautious conservatism may stagnate the individual investor's return, but institutional investors' losses are far greater when caution is "thrown to the wind."

As an aggregate investment, pension funds represent America's largest capital investment for *all* institutions. In 1984, the market value of private pension funds was approximately $623.3 billion. Until 1974 pension fund investment managers had traditionally had more investment flexibility than any other type of investor. Unrestricted by law, they could seek higher than expected yields in so-called off-the-beaten-path investment *media*, particularly since they did not have to worry about liquidity, and tax exemptions allowed them to operate without distinguishing between current income and capital gains. For that matter, they could freely switch overpriced investments into undervalued situations with total disregard for tax consequences. Several of these and other advantages vanished in late 1974 when Congress passed the Employee Retirement Income Security Act—known today by the acronym ERISA.

This legislation created a uniform federal standard for fiduciary conduct in both the establishment and overall maintenance of corporate employee benefit plans. The objective of ERISA was to guarantee employee benefits through sound financial management of pension monies. ERISA contains several provisions that changed the portfolio of the pension fund investor. Prior to ERISA corporations were not legally required to amortize *unfunded* pension liabilities. ERISA converted pension liabilities from the "fringe benefit" category to a legal claim by beneficiaries *against the corporation*. This regulation was made enforceable by federal regulations with standards produced by the new Financial Accounting Standards Board (FASB). If the pension plan should terminate for any reason, beneficiaries are guaranteed that the sponsoring corporation will make good the shortfall. This is achieved through the Pension Benefits Guaranty Corporation, which can attach a lien of up to 30 percent of the sponsoring company's net worth to meet the obligation. To date, this change in liability has apparently had little effect on investment decision making.

Until the Department of Labor clarified the *prudent man rule,* (Section 404 of ERISA), there was great confusion about the risk of loss. Section 404 was initially interpreted to require the minimization of risk on *each security* in the portfolio, rather than the minimization of risk in the portfolio as a *whole*. Section 404 was later interpreted to accept the *total* portfolio approach to pension fund investment management. Small and developing companies rejoiced over this clarification, since they would suffer most from lack of funding by pension investors.

Although investment policy control varies greatly among the various pension fund investors, the trend has been to hire internal portfolio managers in order to return *direct* control of the funds to the sponsoring organization. Companies govern the handling of pension investments by providing their portfolio managers with a set of guidelines. These guidelines identify the minimum total rate of return, minimum annual income requirements, and minimum quality rates for bond holdings. On the other hand, managers usually hold full rein over the rate of negotiated brokerage commissions, volatility or beta of the equity portfolio, and average maturity of the bond portfolio.

In the period from 1982 to 1986, several changes were observed in aggregate pension fund investment behavior:

1. Portfolio returns exceeded actuarial assumptions for an extended time period.

2. Wage gains—the driving force behind pension fund contributions—moderated significantly.
3. Many defined benefit programs were terminated and replaced by *guaranteed* annuities.

Although actuarial assumptions indicated a *required* return of 8.5 percent would be needed to meet future liabilities, most portfolios achieved a 10 percent performance. It is of interest that the better funded plans actually use *lower* assumptions. Portfolio returns are, in general, in *excess* of wage growth. This is a controllable factor that corporations can actually manage throughout their calendar year. Corporations can reduce liability requirements by bond dedication—that is, by designing fixed-income portfolios to match cash flow from coupon payments. These dedicated bond portfolios are currently in use by as many as 17 percent of all companies surveyed. Another 8 percent of those surveyed expect to implement these techniques to reduce past service liabilities from the *total* pension fund liability.

The pressure to terminate benefit programs comes from a number of different contributory factors. Leading the list are *overfunded plans*. These plans provide a source of tempting capital. By refunding benefit obligations with guaranteed annuities, sponsors can recapture significant assets for reassignment into other corporate uses. Couple this with severe employee reduction programs, and you can see how corporations reduce *future* liabilities. Large-scale mergers and acquisitions have also stimulated plan termination in this "shaking out" period of corporate restructuring. These factors are collectively responsible (in part) for the definitive increase in the use of "passive" portfolio management techniques. There is, in fact, a growing belief among pension fund sponsors that risk adjustment measures are more a matter of luck than skill. If this is so, then it is not cost-effective to suffer the high cost of "active" management, with its requisite management fees and transaction costs. These fees and costs erode profitability and *must* be considered in the management of *large* investments.

The most disturbing research into the investment behavior of pension funds has revealed the following:

1. An alarmingly *large* number of pension funds still have no formal statement of investment policy.
2. Even though pension plans differ substantially, their portfolios have *similar* profiles.

3. Portfolio holdings have frequently been plagued with *poorly timed* or *counterproductive* changes in their makeup.

In recent years private pension funds have been extremely volatile. Whereas pension managers purchased a record number of equities during 1982 and 1983, these same managers became net sellers during the bear phase of 1983 and 1984. Rapid swings during the 1980s could and should have been tempered by informed managers—people who understood the theories of risk and return. This improved understanding could have prevented unwarranted changes in long-term planning that were immediately followed by short-term performance problems.

Pension fund trustees have frequently been criticized for holding an excessively conservative posture in their asset allocation policies. Recent creative thrusts have been evidenced by their diversification into real estate, international markets, and oil and gas ventures. Such nontraditional assets have helped increase diversity and refuel the optimism of the trustees.

The Computer as a Tool in Securities Analysis

Where would Wall Street be without paper? Well, the financial world of hard copy is slowly giving way to the flash of numbers on the video display. A correlation could be drawn between the massive growth in trading and the computer. Without its *immediate* on-line verification of transactions, the world of today's financier would be greatly encumbered, if not bogged down, in a hopeless morass of paperwork. The development of electronic computerized markets and other innovative technologies was encouraged by several factors of interest to *all* investors:

1. Competition
2. Government mandate
3. Economic gain
4. Cost efficiencies

Market specialists and traders on the floor at one time made face-to-face transactions. Now, many of these same people sit behind video terminals. When Hurricane Gloria threatened Wall Street in 1985 by closing down SIAC—the Securities Information Automation

Corporation's computerized system network—New York traders became aware of their reliance on this system for stocks and options pricing. It was a good day for Pacific coast investors who use the AutEx systems network. AutEx and Instinet were "up" and so were companies like Jeffries, a Pacific coast investment firm, that took full advantage of SIAC's being "off-line."

Great fortunes have been expended worldwide on electronic equipment in an effort to close the distances between international traders. Losses in computer power can only mean trading "blind," which in today's markets is just about as risky as driving blindfolded! To eliminate this threat, most information services have battery backup or strategically placed off-site/off-location computers that run parallel with on-site systems. Such contingencies are as necessary as a spare tire on a long road trip.

Computers are tools and must *always* be viewed as tools until the day that artificial intelligence equals or surpasses human judgment. By providing calculations in a billionth of a second (or less), computers have replaced error-prone human mathematicians with a reliable source of instant analysis. But the quality of data output is *only as good as the quality of data input!* And, most financial analysts agree, news and rumors are instantaneously reported and quickly heeded. Rumors of takeovers, hints from Congress about trade blockages, or changes in the Federal Reserve money supply are electronic "fodder' for the hungry analysts hovering over their video monitors. Overreaction is actually kindled by the electronic media, and joint ventures such as Inmet (IBM and Merrill Lynch) and Gemco (McGraw-Hill and Citibank) try to maintain the advantage of knowing the domestic *and* global news of finance. The only limiting factor—and perhaps one for which all investors should be thankful—is that the mountain of information created by computers *still has to be interpreted by humans.* But this too will not remain a limitation, since several companies have now undertaken the development of software to "cluge" or compress these mountains into hills of interpretable information.

Computers for the Individual Investor

When the sudden flurry of sell orders becomes a blizzard, the individual investor must know how to weather the storm of financial activity. Failure to take immediate corrective action could result in a serious impact on his or her investment. With the advent of the personal computer and well-established telephone links to trading services, it is now possible for the individual investor to monitor the financial news at home or on the job. The Equalizer, developed by discounter Charles Schwab & Company, packages financial news and quotations along with quotations from Standard & Poor's Marketscope. Fidelity Investors Express, developed by the Fidelity Brokerage Service, links its services to the home computer so that investors can actually enter stock orders, transfer funds, and monitor quotations. This service is provided at a reasonable monthly fee that includes registration and computer connection time.

The home computer consists of *two* basic, yet different, components: hardware and software. The hardware is the actual computer system: the processor (including fixed hard disk and/or one or two "floppy" or rigid diskettes), the video display (color, monochrome, or black and white), the modem (providing a telephone linkage electronically), the keyboard (configured in the style of a typewriter with optional numeric keypad), and an optional printer (dot matrix, impact, which provides typewriter quality print, or laser, which provides the typeset quality of the printed page). The software is the *actual* program of instructions that the processor hardware follows electronically to gather data, process it, and present it to you on the video display. Thus the software is the "brains" of your computer investment, while the hardware is the body in which it resides. Most software environments (as they are called) have been designed for a specific or "target" end user. This means that the computer programmers who design the software have researched the needs of the end user—you and other investors—and have tried to provide the information and data processing that you need to make an informed choice. Needless to say, the software is critical to the success of your interacting with any computer system. Unfriendly software is the least desirable. Most end users prefer a "user-friendly," or comfortable, interactive software environment.

As a rule, you should first identify the software you want, use it for a while, and then find a computer that will run it. Many computer dealers will lend you the software, since it is protected by copyright limiting the number of people per software copy. The best advice is to find someone who has already made a purchase and see if you can use the hardware and software before you buy. Several brokerage and discount firms offer personal computers and software as part of a total package of services they vend at a monthly fee. Do your homework before subscribing to these services. More and more firms will be offering similar services in the coming years, so it is important to know *what* is being offered and the *cost* of the offering.

You can purchase a relatively sophisticated computer system for approximately $5,000, and most software costs between $350 and $500. More expensive computers may *not* be necessary to handle simple programs, particularly those that use interactive information display routines. The price tag goes up as you purchase expensive software that needs larger processor memory (greater than 512 to 640 kilobytes) and a math coprocessor to handle awkward mathematical calculations at a faster pace.

Pick the Right Software and Find the Hardware to Run It

Various combinations of computer hardware and software can perform four major tasks for the investor:

1. Portfolio management
2. Fundamental analysis
3. Technical analysis
4. Option investment

Portfolio management helps investors track the current values for each security. Both realized and unrealized gains and losses can be monitored with comparisons with the broad stock indices, such as the Dow Jones Industrial Average or the Standard & Poor's Index. Portfolio managers can review financial performance using computer software routines that readily access the percentage composition of the investments in terms of overall holdings, major asset category, stock costs, and individual yields. By knowing the investment objective, the beta or risk of stock holdings, total return on a trailing 12-month level, amounts of *un*invested funds, and net realized capital gains (since the start of the year) can *all* be quickly analyzed and adjusted. Access to a data bank and electronic spreadsheets can help investors make informed decisions and help them evaluate their portfolios efficiently to *maintain* their investment objectives.

More sophisticated portfolio managers can tap existing data bases to plot graphs, view prices and volumes of trading, and chart trends. There is no single program, however, that enables you to choose stocks from *fundamental analysis*, set your timing by *technical analysis*, track your individual portfolio, and plan your *option investments*.

Home computers connected via a telephone *modem* to data bases such as the Dow Jones News Retrieval Service can cost as much as $1.20 per minute during regular working hours (prime time), whereas these same services cost as little as $.20 per minute at nonpeak hours with a one-time charge of $75 for a password.[1] Even though it is less expensive to track stocks during off-hours, investors lose the *time-relevant advantage* of making decisions during regular trading hours.

Standard & Poor's offers a disk of 108 key analysis parameters for each of the companies it tracks. The data are updated on a *monthly* basis for timely decision making. For an annual subscription fee of $245, a composite data base of companies that are traded on high-volume exchanges (the New York Stock Exchange with 1,500 companies and the American Stock Exchange with 800 companies) or over-the-counter (OTC) composites of 2,200 companies (annual cost of $490) can be invaluable additions to an individual investor's financial research library.

Media General Financial Services (based in Richmond, Virginia) provides a data bank with the following tapes:

1. Price and volume data, annual income and balance sheet data, and quarterly data summations and key financial and technical ratios are available for some 3,250 common stocks. This product is called Master File.
2. Full 5-year and current-year summaries of 17 key data parameters are available for the same 3,250 issues in a product called Monthly Price History.

Media General offers up to 140 items on all of the New York and American stocks in addition to 830 major NASDAQ/OTC companies. Eight beta factors, 14 relative price ratios, and 41 separate items on price/volume history are computed along with 34 balance sheet data.

Technical analysis is offered to individual investors from the

---

[1]Prices quoted in the text are suggested list prices and may vary with the vendor or package of hardware and software that you purchase. Prices do not include applicable local, state, and federal taxes.

Merrill Lynch Capital Markets Group in a product called Merrill Screen (costing $4,000), which updates data twice a month. Many computers can automatically dial data banks to retrieve data requests in a matter of minutes. They have software that tracks the historical patterns of stocks, price and sales volumes, and other key issues that highlight trends in individual stocks or a group of stocks. One of the limiting factors in tapping data bases for many of these services is that individuals must master the programming language in which information can be retrieved. The second problem is choice: which data base to use with *hundreds* of them available?

In addition, although computers can search through hundreds of thousands of entries in *seconds,* the information gathered will be of little or no basic value to the researcher unless the computer is given the "proper" search routine. It is, therefore, necessary to select the data base(s) essential to the needs of the investor.

On the current market, increasing numbers of software packages are becoming available for IBM and Apple computer systems.[2] Although we do not endorse either of these companies, we must admit that they do offer end users one of the most flexible hardware and software environments available to investors today. Although Ashton Tate's dBASE III (costing around $685) is holding its own as the current favorite data sorter, Javelin Software's offerings avoid the language barrier users face with dBASE III. Javelin is almost $200 less than the Ashton Tate program. The Symantec Q & A also uses "natural language" commands as does Ansa Software.

Spreadsheets are in vogue. Properly designed on a one-time basis, they offer users a chance to monitor performance by updating a few data entries. Instead of starting anew each time an investor wants to evaluate stock performance, the Lotus 1-2-3 program (trademark of Lotus Corporation) provides a spreadsheet *framework* that can be used to profile each stock in a portfolio as well as the *entire* portfolio. Depending on the type of spreadsheet capabilities users need, Lotus offers a range of products that cost between $250 and $495.

Users must be familiar with the principles of basic accounting to maximize the power of spreadsheet analysis. Some knowledge of basic algebraic equations is also desirable, since each "cell" of a spreadsheet is considered a variable that can be handled in terms of an equation, e.g., CELL46 = CELL2 + CELL4 + CELL 29.

[2]IBM is a registered trademark of International Business Machines. Apple is a registered trademark of Apple Computers.

2
Assessing Risk

Risk in Purchasing Power

Unless they are "high rollers," most people who visit the casinos in Atlantic City, New Jersey, or Las Vegas, Nevada, enter the games they play with clear-cut financial objectives. Once the roll of quarters they obtained on the bus ride is gone, $10 or $20 later, unless they are on a winning streak, casual players leave the casinos for more profitable fun in the fine restaurants or the fascinating shops that surround the gambling palaces. Most people are risk averters and, like those casino visitors, seek safe investments that won't lose much more than the original investment made.

Investors also hope to get current income and/or capital gains from an *increase* in the earnings and assets of the corporations in which they have made their investments. Obviously if it takes 10 years to achieve only a 60 percent return on investment (including the reinvested dividends), but the price level during this interval has risen over 100 percent, the investment is clearly losing purchasing power.

On the whole, common stock prices have exceeded the growth of inflation in the U.S. economy. But, if shorter periods are examined, one finds that inflation has often outrun common stock returns. The risk of purchasing power loss must, therefore, be examined and dealt with when equity in an investment is considered on the basis of the *total* return.

In many cases, investors have been disappointed in stock investments as a "hedge against inflation." Over a 10-year period the rate of inflation increased steadily through 1982, when a decline began. Typical risk averters will *not* buy bonds during periods of inflation, since bond prices tend to fall as interest rates rise. In a recent study by Ibbotson and Sinquefield (updated by CDA Investment Technologies, Inc.), the historical data show that during relatively short holding periods of, say, one year, common stocks, corporate bonds, government bonds, and Treasury bills performed *equally* well in relation to inflation that occurred during the same period. If the holding period is lengthened to 5, 10, or 25 years, common stocks not only gained *more* than inflation took away but also increased to a much greater degree than *all* other assets combined.

Figure 2.1 shows the performance of common stocks versus the cost of living between 1897 and 1985. The scale on the vertical *y* axis measures both the relative percentage increase in the Dow Jones Industrial Average, which increased 2,855 percent over the period,

FIGURE 2.1   Common Stocks and the Cost of Living, 1897–1985

and the Consumer Price Index of the Bureau of Labor Statistics, which increased 1,162 percent. It is apparent that common stocks, indicated by the solid line, provided an effective hedge against inflation, indicated by the dashed line, over this period. Note, however, that in some shorter periods where the market suffered sharp declines, the opposite was true (1906 to 1914, 1937 to 1942, 1946 to 1949, 1966 to 1974, and 1980 to 1982).

When adjusted for inflation, the actual return on common stocks, although more volatile than long-term corporate bonds, government bonds, and U.S. Treasury bills, showed positive returns in over 66⅔ percent of all years examined.

Economic Considerations

In a prospective analysis, Ibbotson and Sinquefield offered a forecast based on their historical analysis of financial performance:

> The compounded inflation rate is expected to be 6.4 percent per year over the period 1976–2000 compared to the historical compounded inflation rate of only 2.3 percent over the period 1926–75. The expected compounded return on common stocks for the period 1976–2000 is 13.0 percent per year. Stocks are expected to have a compounded return of 6.3 percent after adjustment for inflation. . . . The nominal compounded annual returns from maintaining either a 20-year maturity government bond or a 20-year maturity corporate bond portfolio are expected to be 8.0 percent and 8.2 percent, respectively, from 1976–2000. . . . The inflation adjusted returns are expected to be 1.5 percent per year for long-term government bonds and 1.8 percent for long-term corporate bonds. . . . The nominal Treasury bill rate is expected to be 6.8 percent per year, compared to the expected 6.4 percent compounded inflation rate, thus producing a very low inflation adjusted Treasury bill return (real interest rate).[1]

Widespread acceptance of a 60-year data performance profile has given the Ibbotson and Sinquefield forecast great credibility, although caution must be applied to avoid overreliance on these trend analyses. Depending on the period analyzed and the indicators

[1] R. G. Ibbotson Associated, Inc., *The Stocks, Bonds, Bills and Inflation Yearbook* (Chicago; updated edition Silver Springs, Md.: CDA Investment Technologies, Inc., 1985).

that are chosen for the analysis, risk and return studies can be contradictory. Depending on the choice of variables, it could be estimated that market equity risk premiums (the difference between the market return and the risk-free return) can range from as low as 0.9 percent to as much as 24.9 percent per year!

What Effects Do Interest Rates Have on Risk?

Fixed-income type securities experience price depressions as interest rates rise. This effect was evidenced in the late 1970s and early 1980s when the combination of high nominal interest rates *and* high inflationary momentum produced real interest rates that were far in excess of the "historical norms." It was noted during this period that the interest rates were very *variable* too. This scenario created great *volatility,* which is not quite the same as interest rate *uncertainty.* The Federal Reserve Board noted that it is the *uncertainty* that matters, since risks involving an unexpected loss or gain have a greater impact on overall economic decisions.

It can be stated that volatile interest rates substantially *reduce* spending on interest-sensitive investments. Several factors contribute to this reduction, including interest rate deregulation, unpredictable or volatile money supply growth, uncertainty about the general policies of the Federal Reserve Board, and inflation expectations. The uncertainty of interest rates contributes to an increase in cash holdings since it is more difficult to forecast future securities prices, while the risk of capital losses grows. In an effort to reduce this risk, investors tend to hold on to short-term near-cash investments, and *money* itself (in money market accounts) becomes a holding in portfolios, since even though it offers less *return,* it simultaneously offers less interest rate *risk.* This is evidenced by an increase in money market deposits and/or money market mutual funds, which although they have market-*related* returns, also experience minimal or no interest rate risk. In the attempt to offset spiraling interest rates, the Federal Reserve has (on occasion) increased the money supply. Commodity inventories become more attractive as the uncertainty about nominal interest rates mirrors the uncertainty about inflation.

A study of investor attitudes during fluctuations in interest rates suggested that low-beta stocks attract investors far more when interest rates *fall* than when the rates *climb.* Investors are also more apt to take greater risks when interest rates are in an upsurge, but these same investors turn to lower risk portfolios as interest rates plummet. Corporations take advantage of declining interest rates by cashing in on corporate bonds that pay high interest yields, so that they can benefit from issue refinancing at lower rates. Investors in these bonds have little or no refuge from these actions.

Business Cycle Forecasting—Risky Business?

Business economists have a penchant for describing the business cycle with an "individualized" flair. A student of investment analysis must account for the "trendy" attitudes of these economists and discover the *intent* of the analyst. There are a seemingly *endless* number of cyclical fluctuations in the business cycle. For over half a century, the National Bureau of Economic Research (a private, non-profit organization) has sponsored several studies on the chronology of the business cycle. Their studies have shown that 10 complete cycles have occurred since 1933. Roughly, then, one cycle occurs about every five years. By comparison, in the preceding 150 years there were 34 cycles, or one about every four years. Although the frequency of cycles has decreased, no two business cycles have been *exactly* the same. Futhermore, the timing of the cycles has no predictable peaks and troughs.

Interest rate cycles and the periodicity of stock prices are closely related to the tides of general business activity. It can be said that, in general, interest rates rise as the business cycle matures. An analysis of the business cycle and the performance of stocks shows that the ability to forecast turning points in the business cycle greatly improves the ability to predict major turning points in the level of stock prices. This should not be misconstrued to mean that every bear market must be paralleled by an economic recession. Stock prices tend to decline prior to a deceleration of economic growth, which does not always signal a recession.

Price changes of individual stocks examined over short periods can indicate the degree to which these stocks have been under or over prices *prior* to a turning point in the market as a whole. Forecasts of relative price changes mirror expected changes in the prosperity of different industries, and it can be shown that some groupings of industries actually gain in the years when the overall market declines. From a historical perspective, office and business equipment, electric utilities, soft drink companies, and tobacco company stocks have performed in this manner at different times. The cyclical nature of stocks and the tracking of the industrial life cycle are covered in a later chapter, but it is important to observe the close association between economic performance and risk on stock performance.

Analysts have suggested that changes in the regulation of financial markets will affect the historical relationship between the tracking of business cycles and movement in the stock market. Over the last decades, monetary policy has been the primary indicator for business cycle analysis, since changes in overall monetary aggregates are the major contributory factor to the cyclic activity of the economy and inflation rates. The Federal Reserve's concern with money supplies has given support to this observation. Carl Walsh has presented a view on the "new" business cycle. He believes that recent emphasis on money has been "misplaced."[2] Walsh argues that the supply of raw materials, technology, and, in general, the business cycle have influenced consumption, production, and saving so as to effect a "new" equilibrium. Careful study of leading economic factors is invaluable in restricting uncertainties over business risk. It should be mentioned that even though these timing relationships have a historical stability within fairly wide ranges, there are no guarantees that the future will be without change.

Strategy for Individual Investors

As we have stated in our other publications, securities analysis is simply the application of common sense in conjunction with certain key mathematical ratios that assist in the decision to buy, hold, or sell certain stocks. The mysterious aura that surrounds the world of securities analysis unravels as you become familiar with the specific tools and techniques of the trade. It is not as remote and complex as some have led you to believe. Most of us who have purchased a home had the same misgivings about the process of mortgage acquisition and securing of title. But, after the first purchase, many of us have shared our expertise with younger first-timers. Understanding the jargon of investing is important. The New York Institute of Finance

---

[2]Carl E. Walsh, "New Views on the Business Cycle—Has the Past Emphasis on Money Been Misplaced?" *Federal Reserve Bank of Philadelphia* (January–February 1986).

has a publication to help in this matter. Entitled *Guide to Investing,* it provides an authoritative introduction to securities investing.

Your relationship with a brokerage firm and a general understanding of your investment goals are the keys to success in obtaining the appropriate *mix* of investments. If you have not already done so, spend some time with your banker or accountant to determine your net worth. This analysis of your current assets and liabilities will give you the necessary direction for an informed strategy. Next, develop a cash flow statement that lists all your income and expenses. It may be difficult to project all income and expenses, since this depends heavily on your profession and the total number of people in your family who work. Making a reasonable estimate of how your income flows on a monthly, quarterly, and yearly basis will greatly assist you in formulating your strategy, however.

Next, draw up a will. This is the one thing that should not be overlooked in financial planning. Although many people are hesitant to make a will, it is *not* a commitment to die, but merely a plan of what is to be done with your money when you *do* pass on. As a *living* document, the will provides a system for planning and managing assets in order to protect the ones you love and reduce the burdens of tax liability. An attorney will assist you in drawing up a will. The fee in most states ranges from $250 to $400 for a "basic will," but it will cost more if there are greater individual holdings. The will should be reviewed periodically (let's say on a biannual basis) to ensure its accuracy and propriety.

Evaluate life and disability insurance requirements. It is not uncommon for a breadwinner to carry $250,000 to $500,000 in life insurance. The best buy for younger investors is a "term" insurance policy, since it provides the most protection at the lowest cost. Older investors can have a combination of term and whole life policies, depending on family size and the age of the head of the family. Many whole life policies have attractive payouts at retirement. Consult a reputable insurance company/agent to discuss these life insurance options.

Disability insurance coverage can be included in many employment packages, but portability between companies is limited, if not prohibited. When you purchase the policy, make certain that it contains a clause that makes it "noncancellable and renewable." Take the time to compare cost and companies, and be certain that you understand the coverage provided *before* you sign.

Plan now or pay later.

Establish an emergency cash fund. Set up money in the form of a money market savings account or savings bonds to cover the unexpected emergencies that arise in families. In most cases this fund should contain $2,500 to $5,000, although individuals of greater wealth should consider higher amounts with an equivalent of six months to a year of *net* earnings. Examine the year-end net earnings on your wage statement or income tax to determine what you need to set aside for six months to a year for this purpose.

Before embarking on any financial plan, do *not* omit any of the recommended steps, even when your net worth shows an accumulation of assets that could provide financial security. Once these steps have been taken, determine your individual investment objectives. We have already covered these in Chapter 1 of this book.

Once you earn money, you want to *keep* it. In today's complex world of tax revision and reform, you must consider steps that will avoid risk of loss to taxes. Individual Retirement Accounts (IRAs) were once in vogue, but the changing tax laws no longer make them as attractive a shelter as they were initially portrayed to be. For most investors the 401(k) plan remains one of the few viable avenues for sheltering income. Most employers have such plans. In essence, 401(k) plans allow an employee to authorize a certain amount of money to be deducted from his or her salary *before* taxes are taken out, thereby reducing the employee's adjusted gross income. Some employers match the amount or contribute an amount based on a sliding scale. It is possible to borrow against these plans. For this reason, 401(k)s are becoming more numerous as individuals seek an alternative to the IRA. It is imperative that you consult with a tax adviser before deciding which type of income sheltering you should use.

Tax laws have also changed on capital gains. In addition, new legislation on the Uniform Gift to Minors Act governing the gift of financial assets to minor children has *both* positive and negative aspects that you should discuss with your tax adviser.

One of the most profitable ways to shelter income is often also one of the most overlooked: namely, self-employment. But, I already have a *full*-time job you may say. Have you considered a *part*-time business of your own? There are dozens of business-related expenses that can serve as tax shelters, even in light of the major revisions to the self-employment deductions. Turning a hobby or other skill you may have into a business may have strategic benefits for reducing gross annual earnings, where it counts, *before* taxes. Again, however, we advise that you consult a tax adviser before undertaking these ventures.

Portfolio Management for Individual Investors

Individual investors have the same management choices as larger institutions in deciding how to allocate their assets. There are thousands of asset allocation models and millions of portfolios. Which one is right for you? In later chapters we will discuss the basic accounting principles for reading financial statements and give specific examples of financial statements for small and large corporations. We will also show you how to perform the basic earnings math that will key you into the buying signs. You will then learn about all the different types of common stock and how to calculate the value of these stocks. Once you have learned the basics, we will show you the industrial life cycle and explain how cyclical variation plays a vital role in a company's earnings and return on equity. Then, we will introduce the "hard stuff"—the analysis of breadth of market, trading volume, and supply/demand analysis. We will familiarize you with the "jargon" of the investor, odd-lot trading, short selling, specialists' sentiment, and mutual fund cash positions. Before you begin trading, you will understand put and call indicators and have an overview of price charts and stock selection techniques used by the big timers. Then, we will examine the tools and indicators: bar charts, fundamental Dow theory, moving averages, point and figure charting, and relative strength. We will even give you the no-nos of insider trading. But this chapter will give you the strategy and the ability to make the tough choices to achieve your targeted rate of return.

First, don't go it alone in the beginning! Even small investors can lose big dollars by trying to do it all themselves. As we mentioned earlier, we are trying to help you make informed choices when you are asked to do so. One of the most courageous things a beginning investor can do is to admit that he or she needs the help of experts to make decisions. But, once a model for the investment portfolio has been presented, the job of monitoring its progress calls for a dual-control device. You know how it's doing, and when it does not meet your expectations, only *you* can change it. We hope that this book will serve as a guide to your decision to change, not as a guide to change itself!

Several publications provide a periodic model to assist investors in adjusting their asset mix. This is done to help plan the disposition of the portfolio in an attempt to balance risk and return during changing market conditions.

Here's how it works. What is your annual target percentage rate of return on your investment? Let's say it is 11 percent. Table 2.1 contains an asset model for the long-term investor.

The model contains five columns. The first is the targeted annual percentage rate of return ranging from 8 percent to 14 percent. The next three columns indicate what proportion of your portfolio should be invested in a particular asset. For example, as of April 1986, a mix of Treasury bills, long-term bonds, and stocks would have been able to deliver your 11 percent annual target if you had allocated your assets with 15 percent in Treasury bills, 45 percent in long-term bonds, and 40 percent in stocks. The fifth column is the standard deviation (S.D.) of this strategy mix, plus or minus ($\pm$) 3.9 percent for this example.

The standard deviation provides an indication of the confidence associated with the investment strategy. In general, one standard deviation has a confidence of 64 percent, which means that 64 times out of 100 events, it will be true, while two standard deviations (equal to two times the stated standard deviation) moves the confidence to 95 percent, meaning that 95 times out of 100 events, it will be true. To stretch this analysis just one more step, plus or minus

TABLE 2.1   **Asset Model: Projected Portfolios for Long-Term Investors**

Annual Target Percentage Rate of Return	Treasury Bills	Long-Term Bonds	Stocks	Standard Deviation
14%	0.0%	5.0%	95.0%	9.0%
13	0.0	25.0	75.0	7.0
12	0.0	45.0	55.0	5.2
11	15.0	45.0	40.0	3.9
10	30.0	45.0	25.0	2.7
9	65.0	20.0	15.0	1.7
8	80.0	20.0	0.0	1.2

three standard deviations gives a confidence of 99.7 percent. To be 95 percent sure of the mix needed to deliver the 11 percent yield, the range of the mix in each category would be as follows:

Annual Target Percentage Rate of Return	Treasury Bills	Long-Term Bonds	Stocks
11%	7.2 to 22.8%	37.2 to 52.8%	32.2 to 47.8%

QUESTION

Examine the remaining annual target percentage rates of return and determine the range of mix in each category for all yields to 95 percent confident. [Keep in mind that negative percentages calculated (values less than 0.0 percent) are meaningless, but values greater than 0.0 percent, e.g., 0.0 percent + 7.8 percent, would be listed as a 0.0 percent to 7.8 percent mix.]

ANSWER

TABLE 2.2   Asset Model: Projected Ranges of Portfolios for Long-Term Investors at +2 S.D. (95 percent Confidence)

Annual Target Percentage Rate of Return	Treasury Bills	Long-Term Bonds	Stocks
14%	0.0 to 18.0%	0.0 to 23.0%	77.0 to 100.0%
13	0.0 to 14.0	11.0 to 39.0	61.0 to 89.0
12	0.0 to 15.6	34.6 to 55.4	44.6 to 65.4
11	7.2 to 22.8	37.2 to 52.8	32.2 to 47.8
10	24.6 to 35.4	39.6 to 50.4	19.6 to 30.4
9	77.6 to 82.4	17.6 to 22.4	0.0 to 2.4

Once the percentage mix is established, you must select the securities in each category. Professionally managed portfolios provide the safest strategy for selection of assets, although long-term trends have demonstrated that there is a significant shift to individuals making their own investments. If we examine the period from 1972 to 1985, we see that individuals have been net sellers.

In the same time frame, mutual funds grew sharply, stimulated by both the individual desire for bond funds and IRA contributions. Ironically, part of individual disenchantment with the stock market was self-inflicted concentration on too few issues without cognizance of the risk involved. Another group of investors, commonly referred to as the "jumpers," tend to shift investments, strategies, and financial objectives too quickly. Great expectations, unwillingness to accept mistakes, and plummeting into "deals" without knowing the financial consequences have driven individual investors to mutuals as a means of fulfilling their expectations on return.

Mutual Funds—The Key Is Pooling

One of the most common joint financial ventures is the mutual fund company. By providing investments on behalf of both individuals and small institutions, mutual funds deliver performance to investors

FIGURE 2.2 **Changes in Individual Stock Holdings (Purchases Less Sales, Including Equity Mutuals)**

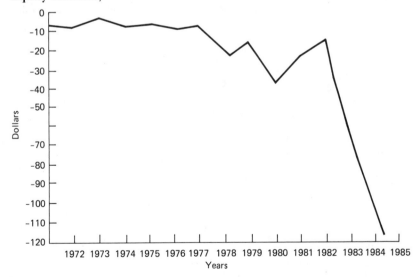

with similar financial goals; pooling is the key to their operation. By pooling his or her stake with the resources of thousands of other investors, the individual investor can gain access to the expertise of the nation's "top" money managers as well as benefit from the wide diversification of ownership afforded in the securities market.

By investing this large pool of monies in a diversified group of stocks, bonds, and other types of securities that have been selected from a broad base of industrial and governmental sources, mutual fund managers seek to invest in those areas that fit the financial objectives of the "fund." Extensive research enables these professional money managers to make informed decisions on when to buy, sell, or hold on to their investments. For the most part, mutual funds are actively managed portfolios. Here's the bad news: One-third of mutual fund managers indicated in a recent survey that they did not have formal practices for evaluating the success of their selections, and only a few of them could describe how performance was measured. If this sounds familiar, it should. The dilemma of the individual investor is often reflected in the practices of larger investors.

With well over 1,000 separate mutual funds to choose from at year's end in 1985, there has been a trend to focus investments on specific sectors such as energy, health care, financial services, electronics, precious metals, and chemicals. Even though these specialized funds tend to be more volatile than diversified portfolios, they have a certain appeal to investors who believe these specialties can be "picked" at certain times or to investors who want to participate in a particular sector by buying individual stocks. A growing number of market services claim to be able to predict when investors should shift in and out of specified "sectors." In a *Fortune* article in April 1985, Mike McFadden reported that investors should be aware that 17 out of the 25 worst performing funds in 1985 were sector portfolios. This observation reinforces our earlier diatribes concerning the risk that accompanies a lack of diversification.

Table 2.3 lists the most common types of mutual funds available.

When individual investors determine the level of risk they are willing to assume, it is possible for them to create a diversified portfolio by combining large, no-load common stock mutuals in a creative mix of risk-free assets or margin purchases. Table 2.4 shows how this type of investor could diversify his or her mutuals portfolio. Repeated studies have shown that mutual fund investors are *not* risk takers. Portfolio theory provides the most effective framework in which individuals can execute investment policy. Placed in its proper

TABLE 2.3   Types of Mutual Funds

Type of Fund	Objectives and Strategies
Aggressive growth funds	Seek maximum capital gains as their investment objective. Current income is not a significant factor. Some of these funds may invest in stocks that are somewhat out of the mainstream such as fledgling companies, new industries, and companies that have fallen on hard times. These funds may also use specialized investment techniques such as option writing or engage in short-term trading.
Growth funds	Invest in the common stock of more settled companies with a longer track record, but their primary aim is to produce an increase in the value of their investments rather than a steady flow of dividends.
Growth and income funds	Invest mainly in the common stock of companies with a longer track record that have the expectation of a higher share value and also have a solid record of paying dividends.
Precious metals funds	Invest in the stocks of gold mining companies and other companies in the precious metals business and sometimes in precious metals futures and options on futures.
Government National Mortgage Association (GNMA) or Ginnie Mae funds	Invest in government-backed mortgage securities. To qualify for this category, the majority of the portfolio must always be invested in mortgage-backed securities.
Corporate bond funds	Much the same as income funds, these seek a high level of income. They do this by buying bonds of corporations for the majority of the fund's portfolio. The remainder of the portfolio may be in U.S. Treasury and other government agency bonds.
Municipal bond funds	Invest in bonds issued by local governments such as cities and states that use the money to build schools, highways, libraries, and similar civic properties. Interest earned on these securities is not taxed by the federal government. The mutual fund buys the municipal bonds and then passes the tax-free income through to the fund's shareholders.

Type of Fund	Objectives and Strategies
Balanced funds	Generally have a three-part investment objective: (1) to conserve the investor's initial principal; (2) to pay current income; and (3) to achieve long-term growth of both the principal and income. They aim to achieve this by owning a mixture of bonds, preferred stocks, and common stocks.
Income funds	Seek a high level of current income for their shareholders. This income may be achieved by investing in the common stock of companies that have good dividend-paying records. Often, corporate and governmental bonds are also part of this portfolio.
Option/income funds	Seek a high current return by investing primarily in dividend-paying common stocks on which call options are traded on national securities exchanges. Current return generally consists of dividends, premiums from writing call options, and net short-term gains from sales of portfolio securities.
U.S. government income funds	Invest in a variety of government securities. These include U.S. Treasury bonds, federally guaranteed mortgage-backed securities, and other governmental notes.
Single state municipal bond funds	Work like other municipal bond funds except their portfolios contain the issues of only one state. The advantage for a resident of that state is that the income is free of both federal and state taxes.
Money market mutual funds	Invest in the short-term securities sold in the money market. (The money market is where large companies, banks, and other institutions invest their surplus cash for short periods of time.) In the investment spectrum, these are generally the safest, most stable securities available; they include Treasury bills, certificates of deposit of large banks, and commercial paper (the short term IOUs of large U.S. corporations.)
Short-term municipal bond funds	Invest in municipal securities with relatively short maturities. They are also known as tax-exempt money market funds.

SOURCE   Investment Company Institute.

TABLE 2.4   Individual Portfolios and Risk

	Type of Investor		
	Conservative	*Capital*	*Speculator*
Assigned beta	0.75	1.20	1.50
Percentage of portfolio in risk-free assets	25%	0%	0%
Percentage of portfolio on margin	0%	20%	50%
Percentage of portfolio in a package of large no-load mutual funds	75%	120%	150%

perspective, the framework is neither foolproof, nor does it eliminate the need for careful risk/return judgments among different asset classes and individual securities. These types of judgments must be made by informed decision making about future uncertainties. Although past relationships may provide the "best" direction, they are merely part of the "process" that maximizes investment opportunities so as to improve on the traditional techniques. Portfolio theory enables investors to evaluate their performance systematically with expectation, for without such evaluation it is difficult, if not impossible, to achieve an acceptable return. In spite of all its imperfections, portfolio theory continues to prove itself as a landmark in the history of financial control.

3
Market
Views

One key assumption in modern capital market theory is that the market is efficient because it is composed of a large number of rational, profit-seeking, risk-averting investors.

The Efficient Market

Most changes that affect the performance of a single stock are communicated quickly throughout the entire community of investors. These changes are rapidly reflected in the prices of stocks. Given these timely adjustments in value, investors should expect that stock prices will follow the developments and will be about the same or very close to the valuations made by all investors who hear any news that affects stock prices. Since the market is capable of quickly incorporating new developments, it is said to be "efficient" in the sense that at any given point in time stock pricing will reflect any valuation changes, all factors being considered. Efficient market theory credits this basic tenet. It follows then that changes in the growth of the money supply that affect interest rates should also be expected to have an impact on market pricing.

Securities analysts are the eyes and ears of an efficient market. Investigative probing and research by curious analysts turn rumor and hypothesis into rational stock-pricing strategies. Through collective action and a near chain reaction to trends, securities analysts determine future prices of stocks. Although momentary deviations from the actual or intrinsic values assigned to stocks may occur, those who espouse the efficient market theory truly believe that these mispriced securities are fleeting.

Destabilization of the efficient market must be considered as a possibility, however. What are the key factors that may lead to destabilization? In addition to the disappearance and failure of some of this country's most prestigious brokerage firms, one factor is the takeover by computerized automated systems. Automated systems respond quickly to tolerances that have been built into them causing price launches and tremors in stock pricing, which lead to volatility.

In addition, on the competitive side, commercial banks and insurance firms are now capable of moving massive blocks of securities in an effort to seize an immediate return. An international securities market is now a reality as a result of rapid satellite communications between exchanges. This added trading capability has contributed to surging share volumes as multinational corporations participate in the trading arena with their fluctuating currency values.

It is no wonder, therefore, that the U.S. government has taken such an active role in regulating a securities market that is now global in scope. The Securities Investors Protection Corporation (SPIC) and the expansion of the National Association of Securities Dealers Automatic Quotation System (NASDAQ) are just two examples of government's effort to control the evolution of the securities market.

This chapter focuses on functional changes that have been made in the exchanges in order to provide the *best* possible trading system for investors. It is important to understand how these changes have deemphasized the individual investor. Government's participation in the deregulation of commissions and the rapid growth of institutional power and funds have changed the game plan for trading in an international market. The introduction of new financial products, coupled with the increased volume of trading activity and decreased distances between national and international investors, has also made a difference. Traders are now able to take advantage of time zone differences. They also must deal with national differences in the degree of financial disclosure required, trading requirements, and the permissibility of trading on "insider" information.

The Money Market and the Capital Market

The distinction between the money market and the capital market is crucial to understanding how financial resources are identified and used. Money markets involve instruments such as promissory notes, bills of exchange, commercial paper, and bankers' acceptances. Treasury bills, short-term tax-exempt issues, dealer paper, and negotiable time certificates of deposit are also included in this category. In general, money market funds change hands for as little as one *day*, and usually for not more than *one year*. Who participates in these money markets? Commercial banks, large and small corporations, the Federal Reserve, and U.S. government securities dealers. The funds are large (usually several millions of dollars), and activity in the market is short term. For example, a commercial bank may make a one-day surplus reserve loan to another commercial bank that is short of reserves.

The capital market funnels some of its funds through *specialized* financial institutions, which include insurance companies, pension and retirement funds, and so-called "thrift" institutions. This contrasts strongly with the money market. The actual transfer of funds is often done through such intermediaries as investment bankers, stockbrokers, and securities dealers, although a direct borrower-lender arrangement is possible. Although bonds, notes, mortgages, stocks, and warrants comprise the bulk of capital market transfer instruments, these markets are *creative* in their search for new ways to move assets through securitization. Some examples of the newer forms of capital market instruments include securitized automobile loan receivables, commercial mortgage pass-throughs, and collateralized issues of floating rate notes for the Euromarket.

QUESTIONS

Place an "M" next to the transactions that are related to money market issues and transfers and a "C" next to the transactions that relate to capital market issues and transfers.

_____ Large corporation borrows directly from an insurance company.

_____ Bank of New York floats a 2-week loan from Chase Manhattan Bank for $2 million.

_____ Union Carbide Corporation places a $125 million surplus in Treasury bills for 180 days.

_____ New York State borrows $10 million from Insured Risk Mutuals.

_____ General Motors Corporation borrows $125 million from Investment Bankers Associates, U.S.

ANSWERS

C
M
M
C
C

What Are Primary and Secondary Markets?

The market in which very liquid (easily traded), previously issued securities are traded on an organized exchange is called the *primary market*. The term *secondary market* is used to describe the market in which securities that are not traded on an organized exchange are traded.[1] A new issue, the initial sale of any authorized but unissued security, is called an *initial public offering*.

Organized exchanges offer "physical" marketplaces for trading and maintain a *free, close,* and *continuous* securities market forum. These markets are *free* because they offer trading prices that are governed by the law of supply and demand—in the absence, of course, of illegal manipulation. We say that they are *close* because the range between the bid price and the offering price is relatively narrow. And, they are *continuous* in the sense that all secondary sales are made with relatively small pricing variability. The market prices on organized exchanges are set by hundreds and thousands of

[1]The term *secondary market* is also used to indicate the market in which all previously issued securities are traded among investors.

buyers and sellers represented by thousands of representative buyers and sellers in mini-auctions held daily on the floor of each exchange.

What Is the Over-the-Counter Market?

The term *over-the-counter market* is misleading because there is no counter or physical *market*place where the buyers and sellers meet to trade their products. The *over-the-counter market* is a loose aggregate of brokers and dealers who create a market principally for those securities that are not regularly listed on the organized exchanges. By definition then, the over-the-counter market is a *secondary* market. This market is a complex network of trading rooms linked by the electronic marvels of the telephone, telex, telecommunications, and other forms of electronic data transmission. The name "over-the-counter" is a carryover from past transactions in which shares were, quite literally, sold over the counters of *private* banking houses.

All federal, state, and municipal securities and most bonds are traded over-the-counter. Bank and insurance company stocks are also traded in this secondary market. Prices are determined by bargaining, and the role of the broker-dealer can range from principal in the transaction to agent for the deal.

QUESTIONS

Place a "P" next to the transactions that are related to the primary market and an "S" next to the transactions that relate to the secondary market.

__P__ Merrill-Lynch purchases 10,000 shares of AT&T stock on the New York Stock Exchange.

__S__ Dow Chemical resells $100 million of its $250 million in Treasury shares through Chase Manhattan Bank.

__S__ Marvell Corporation (not listed on the organized exchanges) sells 10,000 shares to its parent company, Teen-Age Comics, through a private banker.

__S__ New Jersey trades a $30 million bond for Newark's highway improvement program to Insured Risk Mutuals in exchange for payment of its premium for the months of July and August on state park lands.

ANSWERS

P S   *wrong!*
S P
S P
S S

The Registered Exchanges

Established in the year 1792, the New York Stock Exchange (NYSE) is the oldest of all the exchanges. Now a thriving corporation, the NYSE has more than 1,366 members who hold *seats* (memberships) on it. The price for a seat on the NYSE has ranged from an all-time high of $625,000 in 1929 to a low of $17,000 in 1942. As of 1986, exchange seats cost approximately $400,000, but these prices tend to vary with the prices of stocks and trading volumes. The NYSE lists securities for more than 1,500 major companies; only those securities *listed* for trading can be exchanged Monday through Friday from 9:30 A.M. to 4:00 P.M. (Eastern time). It would seem logical, then, that traders would take advantage of the time difference between the NYSE and the Pacific Stock Exchange (PCE), which begins trading 4 hours after the opening of the NYSE. Recently, there has been talk about synchronizing the trading hours to eliminate this disadvantage to the NYSE. Unfortunately, there does not seem to be any resolution for international trading transactions, which can be offset anywhere from 6 hours to almost a full day!

The NYSE has equipment that can process 400 million shares per day. Recent high-volume trading has pushed the equipment to the limits, and the historic trading of October 19, 1987—now referred to as "Black Monday"—all but crippled the exchange. The NYSE staff had to work through weekends to deliver a tally of the astonishing $385 billion loss on paper. Paper losses can be as devastating as the real thing, however; in just a matter of moments, tens of millions of stockholders suddenly felt poorer. Losses like those experienced on Black Monday are not a common occurrence on the NYSE, but, left uncorrected, these losses could have turned the growing American economy into a financial wasteland.

The Wall Street panic of October 19 did not limit itself to the NYSE. For example, the London Stock Exchange closed at 1,403.5, some 400 points below its average of 1,800 on October 6, just 13 days before Black Monday.

We are linked in a world economy of exchanges. Any investor who doubted the theory of economic chain reactions no longer questions the impact of the Big Board (NYSE) on the world exchange. How are all the exchanges linked? In addition to the desktop high-speed ticker tape provided by Consolidated Tape System (which is capable of printing up to 900 characters a minute), there are a number of electronically transmitted tickers that brokerage firms can access with a few simple keystrokes on their on-line computerized quotation systems. Veteran traders know the abbreviations for each of the listed stocks by heart—GM for General Motors, NG for National Gypsum, and KO for Coca-Cola Company. They might use jargon for Coca-Cola and call for a status on "Knock Out" (standing for Coca-Cola's abbreviation KO). Some of the abbreviations are derived from symbols that the companies listed abhor. Ask your broker about SLB or HIA nicknames.

What Types of Orders Are Placed on the Market?

Market Order

After a customer places an order at the market, his or her commission broker is authorized to execute the order at the best possible prevailing price or as close as possible to it at the time the order reaches the post where it is traded. As many as 75 to 85 percent of all orders placed in this way are market orders. The market order is more common in stock sales than in purchases for the simple reason that a seller is usually more eager to get action than a buyer is.

Limit Order

In several instances, a buyer or seller can specify the price at which the order can be executed. These are limit orders because the broker is given a mandate to fulfill at the limit, or *better*. For a "buy" order, the broker must execute the order at the stipulated limit or *lower;*

conversely, for a "sell" order, the broker must make the bargain at a price that equals or exceeds the specified limit.

Limit orders have become increasingly sophisticated over the last two decades. It is now possible for the buyer or seller to enter a limit order on a consolidated Limit Order System, formerly known as CLOB (Consolidated Limited Order Book). The limit order is entered electronically and executed when a specified limit is reached on the price. An Electronic Display Book System will accept limit orders and apply a turnaround number for the bid. In some cases a "good-till-cancelled" status can be placed on these orders when they are not fulfilled on the day they are submitted. This allows the orders to carry forward until they are executed or cancelled by the placing broker.

DOT

Member firms can participate in a coordinated electronic ordering system known as DOT (Designated Order Turnaround System). As many as 1,099 market order shares and up to 30,099 limit order shares (in round or odd lots) can be traded. A 3-minute turnaround makes this process *virtually* instantaneous. Approximately 58 percent of all orders are processed in this way, and DOT guarantees all executions reports will be delivered within a 3-minute time frame.

Stop Order

Like the stop payment order you give a bank to halt payment on a check, the stop order helps you protect your money—with one exception. The stop order can be executed on a buy or a sell transaction. Stop orders are classified as "conditional" market orders because they are processed if something happens to jeopardize a "paper profit." Typically, they are used when a stock is climbing and you don't want to miss out on the profit, or conversely in a sell condition, where your stock is plummeting and you don't want to lose your shirt!

EXAMPLE

You buy Citicorp at 31 and it goes up to 51. You would obviously like to continue to hold on to the stock because it is going up, but you would like to protect your gain in the event the market turns downward. What could you do?

You could place a stop order, say, at 41, which is 10 points *below the current* market value. If the market should turn down, you have protected 10 points of your gain without a loss, since once the stock reaches 41, it will be sold automatically, providing you with a 10-point advantage.

Here's another practical example of how to use the stop order. General Motors is currently selling at 62, and you believe that it is going to go up and split (a rearrangement of a common-stock issue by substantially increasing the number of shares outstanding through either a free distribution to or exchange by each stockholder—discussed in Chapter 4). You decide to buy 100 shares of GM at 62 and issue a stop order to sell at 60.

What has this done? You have *limited* your risk! If your research and/or intuition was *wrong,* you would only be out a two-point loss (plus commissions, of course). Thus, the stop order helps you limit your losses.

We add one caution, however. You are never *assured* that you will get out at the *exact* price that you have designated on the stop order, because your broker will sell at whatever price he or she can obtain when the stock takes a sudden plunge. The stop order is complicated by the fact that all other stop orders set at your limit must be executed on a first-entered first-executed basis; therefore the accumulation of sell orders that are set at your limit may not allow you to recover at the stop-order limit you have specified.

Stop-Limit Order or Stop-Loss Order

The stop-limit order is yet another hybrid. This order allows investors to define the maximum *or* minimum price that is acceptable for either a purchase or a sale of stock. If the broker cannot fulfill the order at the specified price *or better,* there is no transaction.

Not surprisingly, the NYSE has become concerned about stop-order placements, since a downward turn of the market could set off a chain reaction of stop-limit orders. Would this lead to financial Armageddon? Perhaps. From time to time, the NYSE has suspended stop-order placements in order to limit or forestall their possible market repercussions.

Stop-limit and stop-loss orders can be entered over a period of a day, a week, a month, or GTC (good-till-cancelled). Typically, *you* specify the time over which the order is to be valid, and only *you* can cancel it unless you authorize your broker to act in your behalf.

Complete Discretionary Order

A complete discretionary order must be given, in writing, to the broker by the customer. It is a power of attorney over your investments and enables the broker to exercise full discretion over the buying, selling, and types of securities to buy or sell. Additionally, the broker gains "complete discretion" over volumes and times to buy and sell. This authority must be approved by a principal or officer of the firm that will execute it in your behalf.

Limited Discretionary Order

Unlike the complete discretionary order, the limited discretionary order limits the firm that will execute your trading to the price and timing of transactions. In all discretionary orders, you should have established a close working relationship with a reputable broker *before* you consider making these arrangements.

Let's see how much you've learned.

QUESTIONS

Match the type of order listed on the left with the brief description given on the right by writing the letter of the description next to the order.

B Stop-limit order
A DOT
D Market order
F Stop order
C Limit order
E Limited discre-
tionary order
G Discretionary
order

A. Approximately 58 percent of all orders are processed with virtually instantaneous turnaround.

B. Enables the *investor* to define a maximum or minimum price that is acceptable for either the purchase or sale of stock; if the broker cannot fulfill the order at the specified price or better, there is no transaction.

C. Buyer *or* seller can specify the price at which the order can be executed.

D. Authorizes the commission broker to execute the order at the best possible *prevailing* price. More common in stock sales.

E. Limits the control of the broker to price and timing of transactions; used by the infirm, the aged, and investors traveling on long vacations.

F. Helps limit your losses under the protection of a "conditional" buy *or* sell option.

G. Broker is in full control of buying, selling, types of securities, volume, and timing.

ANSWERS

B Stop-limit order	C Limit order
A DOT	E Limited discretionary order
D Market order	G Discretionary order
F Stop order	

How Is an Order Placed?

The exchange is a marketplace—it neither buys nor sells your stock. You can think of the exchange as a forum with a physical location and equipment for making transactions; much like a bank, the exchange provides an environment for the "transaction" of business. By use of what is called the *double auction,* a group of prospective buyers and sellers meet to bid on the active market. Since the buying and trading process has grown to such large proportions, it is carried out with an electronic clerk system know as OARS (Opening Automated Report Service), which matches all buy and sell orders that are entered *before* the market opens on each business day. This enables stock specialists to determine the opening prices for stocks. OARS is located floorwide for all issues. The NYSE DOT System (mentioned earlier in this chapter) allows its member firms to send orders *directly* to stock specialists at their trading posts on the market floor. These specialists are exposed to the total flow of transactions for each stock that they are assigned. Video displays constantly deliver the most recent quotations for each stock. Once an order is processed, a confirmation of the transaction is returned to each member firm utilizing the same communications link that delivered it. The American Stock Exchange (AMEX) uses the PER (Past Execution Reporting) System, which is similar to DOT. Other exchanges, including those located in Philadelphia and Cincinnati and the Pacific Exchange, use systems that both route and execute orders. One of the most recent innovations is a system called Touch Trade, which uses a touch-sensitive video display in much the same way as touch-screen automatic tellers carry out banking transactions. Touch Trade enables the originating firm to (1) enter the transaction, (2) report the transaction to its originating firm, (3) send the transaction to the tape, and (4) enter the transaction into the comparison system to check its accuracy; Touch Trade also automatically updates the price quotation for market and limit orders. It is unfortunate that the age-old ticker tape, although conspicuously stationed around the exchange floor, cannot keep up with the speed of the electronically placed orders.

How Is an Order Finalized?

Formed from the clearinghouses of the NYSE, AMEX, and National Association of Securities Dealers (NASD), the National Securities Clearing Corporation continually debits and credits the accounts for each of the completed buy and sell transactions in a single, consolidated bookkeeping process. It has greatly reduced the delivery costs associated with each market. The Depository Trust Company uses an electronic record of all securities (held in street names), which corresponds to the names of brokerage houses.

There are two major trends in the processing of orders today: (1) the *extensive* use of automated equipment, which has *centralized* the market system, and (2) the gradual shift to "certificateless" stock ownership. Originally developed to automate transactions, the Securities Industry Automation Corporation has enlarged its primary mission to include services to the Intermarket Trading System, the Consolidated Tape and Quotation Plan, the National Securities Clearing Corporation, the Options Price Reporting Authority, and the Securities TeleCommunications Organization.

What Roles Do Exchange Specialists Play?

Although the exchange specialists are relatively few in number, they play an important role. Each makes the market for one or more stocks. The exchange specialists have two principal responsibilities: (1) they carry out limit orders that other exchange members deliver to them, and (2) they perform a more involved duty as dealers and/or principals in their *own* accounts.

Specialists maintain price continuity in a more orderly fashion than would occur if they did *not* participate in limiting the price changes between stock transactions. Through this process specialists give strength to the market and provide the liquidity that makes things tick.

Specialists and their assistants or associates are the bookkeepers who staff the trading posts for one or more stocks during trading hours. They act on behalf of other brokers who are not able to be present to process customer buy and sell orders. Specialists assume *total* responsibility for all orders that are turned over to them for processing. Part of the commissions for stock transactions goes to specialists, and many of their earnings come from transactions that they perform for *other* brokers. Since the decisive role of stock specialists requires their "best" judgment in *most* cases, it has often been said that a conflict of interests exists between the specialists' desire to make money for themselves and their objective to make a market. Does this pose an ethical problem? Yes, it does. Specialists' trading practices must be carefully monitored and assessed. There has been some debate over whether stocks should be reassigned to specialists with the best performance records.

The stock exchange has established various rules for specialists with regard to their overall market experience, dealer function, and the capital they own. For example, they are not allowed to execute buy or sell orders for their *own* accounts until such time as they have fulfilled *all* the public buy orders that they hold at a given price. To maintain market pricing, specialists will frequently buy stock at prices *higher* than others are willing to pay. In this way they are able to offer better pricing continuity. You may ask, how is this possible? Here is an example. You be the judge.

EXAMPLE

Matlux Corporation has just sold at 55, and the highest price anyone is willing to pay after this transaction is 54¼ (which is the best *bid*). Specialists who make deals for their own accounts may decide to bid 54¾ (the best *offer*) for 100 shares of Matlux; this makes the quotation 54¾–54¼, thereby narrowing the difference between the bid and offer prices to ½ point. Let us say, for illustration purposes, that a prospective seller wishes to sell 100 shares at best bid (54¾). What has the specialist done to offer the seller a better price?

By making a bid at 54¾—¼ point *below* the current selling price—the specialist has *narrowed* the variation from the last sale by ¼ point. The specialist has accomplished two things: (1) maintained price continuity and (2) offered a *better* price than the best bid.

On occasion, specialists will *sell short*. This means they sell stock that (at the moment) they do *not* own. We shall consider this subject in Chapter 7 when we discuss technical analysis. Specialists must follow a number of specific rules and regulations when they sell short.

As the use of computerized automated systems increased, many specialists feared obsolescence. This fear has been disspelled by the fact that most exchanges have used these systems to *enhance* the role of the stock specialists by making them *more* competitive.

Registered competitive market makers are comprised of two basic groups. The larger group consists of the *floor traders* who hold seats for a fee and assist other brokers with their order processing. A smaller group is made up of *commission brokers* who are employed by member firms who charge them with buying and selling for an individual firm's customers.

What Are the Requirements for Listing on the New York Stock Exchange?

In order to be listed on the New York Stock Exchange (NYSE), a company must meet certain listing or eligibility criteria. These criteria apply whether a company is national or local in exposure. Relative position and standing within its industry and industry expansion intent are also examined to determine a firm's ability to *maintain* its *relative* position. The NYSE imposes the following minimum requirements:

1. *Demonstrated earning power under competitive conditions.* A company must demonstrate earning power of $2.5 million annually (before taxes) for the most *recent* year, and at least $2 million for each of two preceding years.
2. *Net tangible assets of at least $16 million.* Greater emphasis is placed, however, on the *aggregate* worth of the common stock.
3. *Market value of publicly held common stock should equal at least $10 million.*
4. *Publicly held common stock should total at least 1 million shares.*
5. *There should be at least 2,000 stockholders, each with 100 shares or more.*

There is no absolute right to a *continued* listing on the exchange. The NYSE "delists" stocks or suspends a security whenever it deems that trading is no longer advisable. There are many advantages to listing on *several* exchanges, although various independent studies have shown that there is a great rivalry among the various exchanges.

What Are the Requirements for Listing on the American Stock Exchange?

Until 1953 the American Stock Exchange (AMEX) was called the New York Curb Exchange because its members conducted all trading along the curb of Broad and Wall Streets until 1921. The AMEX conducts its business with procedures similar to those of the NYSE. Listing requirements are similar, but the AMEX continues to be comprised of those companies with *less* maturity and "seasoning." Although the AMEX does hold some of the stable, old-line companies, it has *always* served as a proving ground for the Big Board (NYSE). Du Pont and General Motors were listed on the AMEX in their younger days. On average, prices of stocks listed on the AMEX are *lower* than those listed on the NYSE (the AMEX average is approximately $20 per share, whereas the NYSE average is approximately $32 per share). The AMEX has moved as quickly as the NYSE to automate transactions. Until 1976 listing on *both* the AMEX and the NYSE was not permitted. This landmark decision may be considered another step toward a central market system. The Securities Industry Association has advocated the merger of the two exchanges for greater efficiency and cost cutting. Yet another move toward a central market system, this proposal has met with approval from several sides, but one question remains: Who would hold the options market? Since the AMEX has been *very* successful with options, it is not anxious to lose this distinction.

Eighty-seven percent of all stock transactions occur in the NYSE and the AMEX—with 80 percent of the activity in the NYSE and approximately 7 percent in the AMEX. All other exchanges hold about 12 percent of the trading. Companies listed on the AMEX can choose among a list of seven specialists provided by the exchange, whereas the NYSE allows no such choice.

What Are the Regional Exchanges?

There are five separate regional exchanges: the Midwest, the Pacific, Boston, Philadelphia, and Cincinnati. During the previous 10 years, these exchanges have gained from increased shares of securities trading brought about by the Intermarket Trading System (ITS). More than one-third of the securities listed on the regional exchanges now reap the benefits of joint membership with the NYSE and the AMEX. Larger regional exchanges list as many as 600 to 900 companies, which, for the most part, are headquartered in their respective regions.

Eight trading environments belong to the ITS: New York, American, Boston, Midwest, Pacific, Philadelphia, Cincinnati, and the National Association Dealers Automated Quotation System (NASDAQ). Brokers are able to complete trades in *seconds* with specialists, brokers who represent the public, and other market makers. The ITS provides a forum for the best possible price available to the national network of its members. Individual market centers compete for bid and offer stock prices. Stocks listed on the ITS can be assessed for each of the member exchanges regarding the best bid and the best offer.

Cincinnati

Trading on the Cincinnati Exchange is *entirely* computerized. Created as the "test market of the future," Cincinnati carries out its trading nationwide by a computerized system that places buy-sell orders automatically through a computer network. Limit orders are placed electronically, and once the price is reached, transactions are executed electronically. Strict limitations on the Cincinnati Exchange define both the *number of shares* traded and the *individual stocks* that can be traded.

Philadelphia

Gaining recognition for its innovations, Philadelphia holds the unique distinction of being the *oldest* of the exchanges. It began trading *stock options* in 1975 (which now account for more than one-half of its business). Philadelphia is the *only* market for over 75 such options. It trades more than 1,400 multiple listed issues.

Philadelphia enjoys approximately 100 major stock listings and includes some 30 regional stocks that are *not* listed on either the NYSE or the AMEX. Philadelphia pioneered the worldwide linking of trading to the London Exchange when it began foreign currency options. This trading was followed with other currency options including the Swiss franc, French franc, West German mark, Japanese yen, and Canadian dollar. Philadelphia is attempting to promote multinational interest in these options, which would benefit other countries that attempt to secure their interests by avoiding *significant* swings in the *rates* of foreign currency exchange.

Boston

The smallest of the exchanges, Boston has the lowest trading volume and is, by far, the least modernized. Last to be linked to the ITS network, Boston has steadily attempted to attract additional business.

Pacific Coast Exchange

The Pacific Coast Exchange has only 4 percent of the trading volume, but holds a 10 percent market share of NYSE listings. Talk of longer hours and a 100 percent joint stock listing has received the *guarded* attention of analysts who recognize the Pacific's time advantage, which has accounted for significant activity after the Big Board closes in New York.

What Impact Does the Over-the-Counter Market Have on Trading?

As we mentioned earlier, those securities transactions that do not take place on one of the exchanges are called over-the-counter (OTC) transactions. There is no *centralized* place for trading in the OTC market. Varying in size, experience, and general function, *all* registered broker-dealers are allowed to participate in OTC trading. The Securities and Exchange Commission (SEC) authorized the OTC market to trade 25 NASDAQ option listings. The SEC was to review the trading after 1 year, and the verdict is pending as to whether to open additional trading to the OTC membership (as of the writing of this book, no formal opinion has been published).

OTC securities are highly diverse and have a high representation in government and municipal bonds. In addition to trading common stocks, the OTC market also trades bank and insurance company issues. Its emphasis is on high technology corporations. It should be noted that several OTC companies are not easily distinguished from firms listed on the Big Board, AMEX, and regional exchanges. In the process of executing buy-sell transactions, market makers can fulfill orders as either the principal *or* the agent for a public customer.

Stock price differences between the cost for stocks purchased through wholesale dealers and the reselling price (including markup) are *not* a matter of full disclosure to customers. Sparsely traded issues have the greatest spread between bid price and asking quotation. OTC stocks are listed separately on four systems: NASDAQ/OTC, the National Market System, the National List, and the Supplemental List.

How Does the NASDAQ Help Meet
Over-the-Counter Investor Needs?

The National Association Dealers Automated Quotation System—known as the NASDAQ—is a computerized system of communications that collects, stores, and displays up-to-the-second OTC quotations. The NASDAQ ranks third in size on the securities network, with the NYSE and the Tokyo exchange holding first and second place, respectively. In the period from 1975 to 1985, the NASDAQ has experienced a 1,400 percent increase in share volume and a 1,000 percent increase in dollar trading volume. NASDAQ listing standards are comparable to those of the American Stock Exchange, and it follows the SEC standards for disclosure. Pension fund managers in a growing number of states can now trade NASDAQ stocks. The NASDAQ functions on *three* distinct levels to meet investor needs as well as the needs of OTC traders and market makers.

Level 1. Level 1 service is targeted at the *individual investor* who is a client of the various retail branches of brokerage houses. Quotations are current, accurate, and quite visible since they appear on terminals within 5 seconds of their placement. Multinationals have some 10,000 terminals in the almost 120,000-terminal international linkage that offers *last sale price* quotations on an ever-increasing OTC trading volume.

Level 2. OTC *broker dealers and large-volume professional order fulfillment houses* have level 2 units, which have totally automated quotation access.

Level 3. Similar to the level 2 equipment, level 3 units are used by *394 market maker dealers* who can update stock quotations on their individual markets.

Almost three-fourths of all transactions processed through clearing corporations are handled by the Trade Acceptance and Reconciliation Service (TARS). TARS is particularly helpful during periods of high-volume trading activity.

What Is the National Market System?

Now listing over 2,000 issues, the National Market System (NMS) holds the distinction of having share volume equaling *one-half* of the NASDAQ volume. Several high tech corporations prefer OTC listing to retain greater liquidity (discussed later in this chapter). Computer companies such as Intel and Apple qualify for the more rigid requirements of the NYSE, but maintain liquidity positioning through the competition of the multiple market makers. Recent studies have shown a net decrease in the liquidity of companies who move from OTC to *either* the NYSE or the AMEX.

In NMS listings emphasis on corporate earnings and net worth takes precedence over volume. The NMS requires a 4-year record of at least $8 million in capital and surplus with a public float of 800,000 shares, 300 shareholders, and two market makers per issue.

How Does Liquidity Affect Stock Pricing?

In its Winter 1984 issue, the *Journal of Financial Research* (of Texas A&M University) reported that "the average liquidity ratios on the NASDAQ were much greater than those on the AMEX . . . NASDAQ also showed higher *average* liquidity than the Big Board in 8 out of 10 groups." In the study, a liquidity ratio was defined as the dollars required to elicit a 1 percent change in stock price. It was discovered that small company trading of issues worth only several thousand dollars could affect price, while large companies needed $500,000 to $1 million to effect a pricing change.

What Are Discount Firms?

To meet the criticisms of institutions who had to pay the same commissions on large orders as smaller investors were paying for much smaller deals, the SEC abolished years of "fixed" commission rates in May 1975. Since this time, fees for orders placed by *individuals* have jumped, and commissions for orders by the larger *institutional* investors have dropped. What has this meant for the smaller investor? Small investors now pay between 14 and 20 percent more (on average) to process a share, while larger investors now enjoy a 77 percent per share advantage in commission.

The "May Day" action hurt small investors and encouraged the rapid growth of "no-frills" discount firms, which now hold more than 18½ percent of the retail share volume. For smaller investors in both stock and realty markets, *broker* is an appropriate term, since the increase of these middlemen has done more to erode the profitability of the small investor over the last decade than probably any other contributory factor. Charles Schwab & Co.—one of the nation's larger discount firms—has nearly 100 branches and holds over one-fifth of the discount business. By offering sizable discounts for big trades, Schwab has attracted larger transactions. Schwab also has diversified its products by offering several attractive packages for individual retirement accounts, asset management services, and mutual fund trading. Recent studies indicate that younger investors who are attracted to discount firms tend to trade more actively—adding to overall stock pricing volatility.

Do Institutional Traders Add to Pricing Volatility?

Several investigations have shown that discounters play a significant role in *adding* to pricing volatility by increasing the spread between bid and asked prices. It was found that these spreads are particularly pronounced when discounters do not shop around for the best price. This is evident in all trades, but especially in the OTC market. Pension funds consistently push for lower commission rates. Third-party brokers actually specialize in these institutional trades by offering commission rates as low as *2 cents per share*. For stocks considered to be "easy trades" (stocks that always have buyers and sellers), low discounts or rebates are common, while the "difficult trades" do not contribute significantly to this induced volatility. Full-service brokerages get most of the difficult trades and charge the *same* rate for easy or difficult trade executions.

The *Wall Street Journal* reported that commission deregulation has fueled a 61 percent annual turnover rate for professionally managed stock portfolios. Pension funds' demands for rock-bottom commissions and competition from the mutual funds have created an uncertain future for the million dollar brokerages. In the quest for increased capital and broader activity, several brokerages have sold out to corporate giants, such as the American Express Company, the Prudential Insurance Company, and Sears.

The tremendous surge of institutional trading in the early 1980s and the shift to stock control by private pension funds have made the individual investor a dwarf compared to the "block" traders. Block trading has increased dramatically since the mid-1970s. Figure 3.1 clearly illustrates that these trades have more than doubled since mid-1976, while small trades as a percentage of total volume on the NYSE have fallen greatly since 1975 (see Figure 3.2).

Part of the strength of pricing has always rested in the *random* decisions of the small investor. Now, market prices *react* to the *volume* decisions of the large institutional portfolio managers. All these managers have instantaneous access to the same information, and their reactions have a great impact on the market as a whole. Since all institutional managers are rated on their buying and selling records, there is an additional pressure to perform. Surges in market volume can result from the "technically based" institutional sell strategies that are meshed to *pre*determined pricing levels. The market performance is serrated on a quarterly timing cycle, which responds to wide pricing fluctuations as a result of trading the winning and losing stocks in these massive portfolios. Can you believe that institutional portfolios experience an annual turnover of almost 100 percent? That's the truth!

FIGURE 3.1   Block Trades as a Percentage of Total Volume on the NYSE

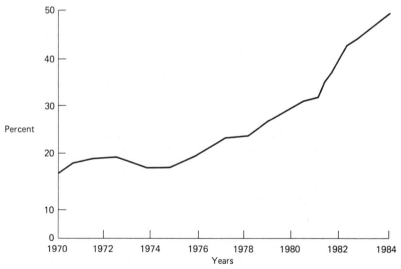

SOURCE *Investment Analysis and Portfolio Management,* New York Institute of Finance, New York, 1987, p. 72.

FIGURE 3.2 Small Trades as a Percentage of Total Volume on the NYSE

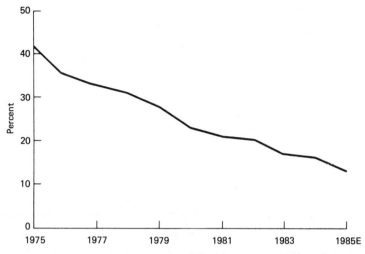

SOURCE *Investment Analysis and Portfolio Management,* New York Institute of Finance, New York, 1987, p. 72.

Review time!

QUESTIONS

Place a "T" next to the statements that are true and an "F" next to those that are false.

_____ Criteria for listing on the NYSE are *not* affected by a company's *relative* position in the industry.

_____ There is *no* absolute right to a continued listing on the NYSE.

_____ The AMEX has classically served as the proving ground for the Big Board.

_____ The AMEX holds only 7 percent of stock activity.

_____ Almost 50 percent of the regional exchanges enjoy joint membership on the NYSE and the AMEX.

_____ Boston is the oldest exchange.

_____ The OTC has no centralized trading.

_____ Sparsely traded issues usually have the widest spread between bid price and selling price.

ANSWERS

F	F
T	F
T	T
T	F

Modern Portfolio Theory and Practice

The desire to quantify risk and its relationship to return has been the unending quest of professional portfolio managers and their clients. In the early 1950s and continuing on into the 1960s, it was possible to gain well beyond calculated expectations as a result of portfolio managers' willingness to take high risks in their investments. For that matter, the entire concept of risk was only in its infancy. At that time there were only broad-based categorizations of investment strategies: *conservative, defensive, growth, income,* and *speculative.* The increasing appearance of data bases on the performance of a large number of diversified portfolios (over a significant time frame) has provided a basis for some new ideas about the investment decision-making process. Advances in the academic community have resulted in modern portfolio theory or capital asset pricing theory.

Modern portfolio theory analyzes risk in tangible quantitative terms and focuses on the problem of portfolio *composition* rather than the more exhaustive analysis of *individual issues* in the portfolio itself. Using concrete objectives, the theory can offer investors explicit advice based on performance, rather than speculation based on trends that do not pass the test of time. Part of the early resistance to the theory was the fear by several groups of managers and analysts that the theory would replace them. On the contrary, its practice has actually created added tasks and enlarged the scope of the portfolio manager and stock analyst.

What Is the "Efficient Frontier"?

Dr. Harry M. Markowtiz presented a group of propositions regarding the "rational" behavior of investors that now serves as the theoretical foundation for the systematic composition of optimum portfolios. Using mathematical modeling and an algorithmic approach to selecting securities, Markowitz was able to show analysts and managers that the purchase and sale of individual securities are significant only to the extent that these decisions affect *overall* portfolio risk and return. Markowtiz was able to explain that weighting the contributions of individual investments to the entire portfolio's financial risk and expected return could serve as a tool for managing the portfolio. In addition, Markowitz was able to show that rational investors must conduct their transactions in a manner consistent with their inherent aversion to absorbing increasing risk *without* compensation by an acceptable *increase* in the portfolio's expected return. For Markowitz, risk is the variability of returns as measured by the standard deviation of the expected return around the mean or average expected return. For the first time, the performance over time was made the key issue; this pioneering step in quantifying investment risk for portfolio planning is the basis for modern portfolio theory.

Next, Markowitz showed investors that they should attempt to *minimize* the deviations from the expected portfolio rate of return by *diversification*. Furthermore, he warned that this diversification had to be examined for security *timing, direction* of performance shifts, and overall *magnitude* of the fluctuations. Quite simply put, expected returns of the elements of the portfolio should *not* all move synchronously *(all in the same direction at the same time)!* The variability of the portfolio's individual components do not sum *directly* to the variability of return.

Variance of portfolios can be illustrated by demonstrating the correlation of returns. Let us assume that we have a two-stock portfolio. In the first case the stocks are "perfectly" and "positively" correlated on their price changes. When stock A moves up, so does stock B with regard to price. Figure 3.3 shows this positive correlation of returns.

By combining these two securities in a portfolio, the variance of the "total" return is *not* reduced. On the other hand, when two securities are *negatively* correlated with regard to their price changes, as shown in Figure 3.4, their movement up and down in the same *proportion* does not affect the *constant* average return, and variances in the portfolio's return are virtually eliminated!

Practical portfolio analysis goes way beyond our simplistic two-stock example, so the mathematics requires an analysis of the covariance of return for *each* issue in the portfolio. The "efficient model" that Markowitz demonstrated used quadratic programming to de-

FIGURE 3.3   Perfect Positive Correlation of Returns

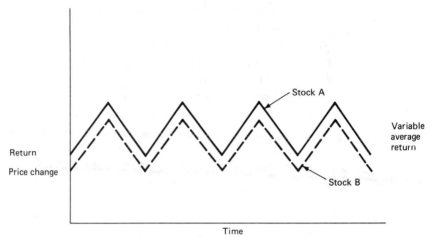

termine a mathematical model of the portfolio. Markowitz was able
to show how portfolios could be contrasted on performance. Graph-
ing the expected return versus the risk (standard deviation of the
expected return) offered an understandable method of comparing
portfolios. In Figure 3.5 we have graphed four separate portfolios: A,
B, C, and D. Note that the y axis (vertical line) graphs expected
return, while the x axis (horizontal line) graphs risk (S.D. of the
expected return). As graphed, portfolio B's expected return is less
than that of portfolios C and D. Portfolio D is the riskiest portfolio,
followed by portfolios A and C, which have identical risk (but

FIGURE 3.4   Perfect Negative Correlation of Returns

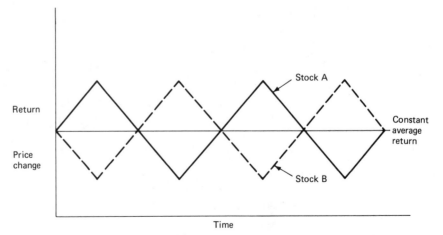

FIGURE 3.5   The Efficient Frontier: Expected Return versus Risk (S.D. of the Expected Return)

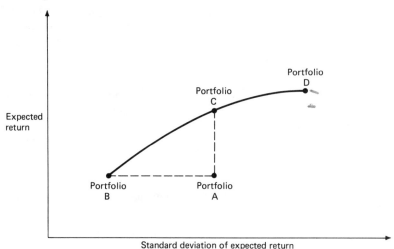

different expected returns), and portfolio B, which has the least risk *and* least expected return.

What are your observations?

QUESTIONS

Place the letter of the portfolio(s) that each of the following statements describes beside the statement:

____ The least efficient portfolio
____ The portfolio with *identical* risk to portfolio A
____ The portfolio with *identical* return to portfolio B
____ Portfolio with the best return for the lowest risk

ANSWERS

A
C
A
B,C,D*

*Depending on risk preferences.

the inc. risk in D is not worth the small inc. in return

∴ B or C dep. on pref.

Here are some comments on our choices:

The least efficient portfolio is portfolio A, since portfolio B can produce the same expected return with lower risk. Portfolio C has the same degree of risk as A but a higher expected return.

Portfolio A and portfolio C have identical risks since they are at the *same* standard deviation of expected return.

Portfolio B has the same return as portfolio A since it is at the *same y* value on return.

Portfolios B, C, and D cannot be compared as to which is "best." All have the highest expected return for a specified level of risk; conversely, these portfolios all have the lowest risk for a specified level of expected return. Thus, the investor's risk preference would determine which portfolio is best. That is, the investor would choose a level of risk (expected return) and select the portfolio with the highest expected return (lowest risk).

In general, most portfolios reside in the middle of this curve, with the fewest at the ends of the curve. Portfolio D delivers the best return, but has a high degree of risk associated with it. Conservative investors would choose a portfolio with B's characteristics, while more aggressive investors would choose portfolio D with higher and yet more variable returns.

Are There Perils and Pitfalls to Markowitz's Theory?

Markowitz's theory also contains certain perils and pitfalls. We will discuss just a few of them here. Keep in mind, however, that the theory *does* provide one of the most practical frameworks for portfolio performance measurement and this alone makes it a wise consideration for all investors.

Pitfall 1. Using the historical perspective of price volatility as a guide, Markowitz has focused on variance as the indicator of possible *future* risk; at a minimum, this requires expected returns to be symmetric. If expected returns are skewed, for example, you are more likely to have large positive returns than large negative returns. Then variance is not the correct measure of risk.

Pitfall 2. The mathematics involved is not easily within the reach of most portfolio managers and security analysts. Although these practitioners are accustomed to evaluating the possible rates of return, they are not statistical wizards who can readily identify covariances among the securities they analyze.

Pitfall 3. Each time the portfolio is evaluated for possible changes, the entire population of securities must be reevaluated for the balance in risk and return. The number of calculations is mind numbing. In a simple analysis of 100 securities, one would have to consider approximately 5,000 covariances. Markowitz offered a simplification of this process by suggesting that analysts look at the returns of each security and compare these to the overall index of market prices. It was this suggestion that led analysts to one of the greatest discoveries in both the theory and practice of portfolio management, the capital asset pricing model and beta.

In addition, the expense of the volume of calculations required for efficient portfolio management under Markowitz's tenets would be prohibitive. We must emphasize, however, that, although Markowitz's theory is flawed by excessive analysis, it remains a milestone: Focused attention on total portfolio risk is fundamental to understanding and controlling return for each client.

Why Is Diversification of Portfolio Assets Crucial to Diminishing Risk?

Diversification diminishes risk because, although the returns of all securities tend to move together, they do not move in exactly the same manner. If all securities moved in exactly the same manner, then diversification would be of no value. Theoretical models and empirical studies demonstrate the effect of diversification; as the number of securities in a portfolio increases, the variance of the return of the portfolio decreases. Since all securities have some similar underlying economic risk factors (for example, beta) and no two securities are expected to move in exactly opposite directions, diversification does not reduce the risk (variance) of the portfolio to zero. The common risk among securities portfolios, the systematic risk of the portfolio, cannot be diversified away.

How Can the Average Investor Take the Smallest Possible Risk to Assure the Greatest Possible Return?

How the average investor can take the smallest possible risk to assure the greatest possible return is an age-old question. Here are some thoughts. Measuring the expected return and riskiness of all possible portfolios of securities is a nearly impossible task. After Markowitz's ground-breaking work in 1959, analysts attempted to look at portfolios with mathematical algorithms or models, but the millions of potential portfolios made this task insurmountable. The rapid growth of computerized modeling techniques that ensued led Professor William F. Sharpe to investigate ways in which a simple model could be used to describe the risk/return trade-off. This model is called the *market model.* It is based on the assumptions underlying the capital asset pricing model.

The relationship between risk and return has given rise to a group of concepts that include the efficient market, random walk, efficient frontier, capital market line, volatility, covariance, beta and alpha analyses, portfolio construction, and performance measurements. All of these concepts have been joined into the capital asset pricing model.

What Is the Capital Asset Pricing Model?

The *capital asset pricing model (CAPM)* is based on two principles: (1) Markets are regarded as being fundamentally in equilibrium. This assumption arises from the fact that the diversification of risk/return *preferences* tends to balance response by this constant and random change. (2) Action and reaction to changing events causes investors to constantly revise their strategies concerning the "expected" rates of return on their portfolios—both on individual securities and the total portfolio composition.

Critics of the CAPM claim it is *impossible* to test the validity of the model, since the market (per se) cannot be defined. If you do not know the dimensions of the *total* market portfolio, you cannot test the theory. Things that are *un*testable are *con*testable!

As the CAPM has been challenged, several modifications have been suggested. Nonetheless the CAPM makes some key assumptions that are worthy of consideration:

1. Although most investors are risk averse, there may be some exceptions.
2. The control of risk is sought via diversification of holdings.
3. Risk/return relations are viewed over *similar* time frames.
4. There is a common view of variance as an indicator of the riskiness of future returns.
5. Borrowing and lending at prevailing risk-free rates (using, for example, a 91-day Treasury bill) enable investors to sell short *without* restriction.
6. Investors can commit any amount of money without affecting the price or rate of return associated with any investment.

It can be seen that several of these classic assumptions may not hold up in practice. Sharpe and others argue that nonetheless they are close enough to reality to enable analysts to consider their impact on security-pricing behavior. The equilibrium of the market as a whole to the pricing of individual securities supports the "fair price" relationship to risk that is associated with *ownership* of securities. Investors cannot hope to earn high returns without increasing risk. Conversely, lowering risk will *decrease* expected returns.

What Is an Optimal Risky Portfolio?

The CAPM does not match the Markowitz scheme with regard to risk adjustments. The portfolio in the CAPM is the entire market. Risk is adjusted by borrowing or lending against a single optimal risky portfolio—the market itself. In the CAPM, the curve of Markowitz's risk/return model is smoothed into a straight *line!* Figure 3.6 compares this capital market line to Markowitz's efficient frontier.

FIGURE 3.6   The Capital Market Line

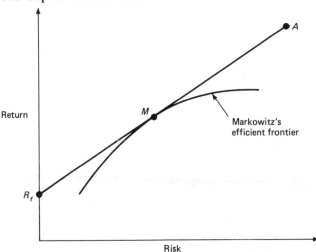

Markowitz's efficient frontier is a trade-off curve in the sense that it is a set of alternative portfolios, each of which maximizes efficiency by providing the greatest expected return at each level of risk. Risk *attitude* determines the point on the curve where each investor is most comfortable. In the Sharpe model, investor risk attitude must be reflected in borrowing or lending against the maximum/optimal risky portfolio—the market. Figure 3.6 illustrates that the CAPM has a point R_f that is the expected rate of return possible from investment in a risk-free asset during a certain time frame. The line segment R_fM corresponds to the various returns that are possible by combining those commitments in risk-free assets and risky assets (represented by the market index). It is possible to have combinations of assets that cover a totally invested position in risk-free assets all the way to portfolios that reflect the market itself. The line segment MA contains investments that yield greater than expected returns, wherein the investor is assumably borrowing at the risk-free rate and is capable of reinvesting borrowed funds in the market—an enviable "leverage" position that offers returns beyond those yielded by the Markowitz model. It is true, but unfortunate, that most investors are not able to achieve returns of this kind, since virtually *all* portfolios are restricted in their capability to borrow. Individual investors are reluctant to do this too.

Theorists have built on Markowitz's work to move away from standard deviation to the beta as the principal measure of risk. By combining many dissimilar stock issues into a single portfolio, the specific component of risk and return is *less for the portfolio than for any of the individual stocks in that portfolio.* The comparative risks of alternative well-diversified portfolios can be assessed by comparing their betas.

Let's turn to the video tape!

Let's replay part of this chapter and see if you can determine where the camera lies. Place a "T" in front of the statements that are true and an "F" in front of those that are false.

QUESTIONS

___F___ In the Markowitz model, most portfolios reside in the low-risk, high-return part of the curve.

___T___ Markowitz advocates variance as the key indicator of possible *future* risk.

___F___ Markowitz would consider the overall index of market prices to be an unacceptable simplification in the analysis of the returns of each security to this "general" index.

___F___ The wider the overall variety of assets, the greater the chances for loss of control for the overall *rate* of return.

___T___ The real interest rate is the difference between nominal interest and the rate of inflation.

___F___ Diversification of risk/return preferences tends to destabilize market equilibrium.

___T___ Market equilibrium supports the "fair price" relationship to risk that is associated with stock ownership.

ANSWERS

F	T
T	F
F	T
F	

4

Reading Financial Statements

Intelligent investment decisions are made after careful consideration of available information: facts about world events, domestic news, industry reports, and corporate announcements. Most investors also rely on financial information released by the company to aid them in their judgments to buy or sell.

Information that comes from the corporation itself is subject to an individual investor's interpretation. A corporation with $1 million in total assets and at least 500 stockholders is obliged to register with the Securities and Exchange Commission (SEC) under the Securities Exchange Act of 1934.[1] These corporations must report significant events and changes as they occur periodically and must file an audited financial statement with the commission annually. At about the same time, similar information is distributed to the company's shareholders. This information is "raw," however, without explanation or analysis. Shareholders and prospective purchasers are expected to know and understand the techniques the company uses to keep the investment community informed. This is often a difficult task because accounting is not a precise science. It is a sophisticated

[1]Exempt from this rule are banks and insurance companies regulated by state or federal authority, whose rules parallel the SEC's anyway. Also excluded from reporting requirements are corporations engaged in religious, educational, fraternal, or certain other enterprises.

art, which uses various methods to present the same basic information and arrive at different conclusions.

Accounting practices vary from company to company, even within the same industry. Frequently, the difference in approach depends upon management's judgment. Sometimes it depends upon the preferences of the auditor. In any case, anyone who analyzes such information should realize that these documents are part fact and part opinion.

Nevertheless, valuable insight into the health and wealth of a corporation is often readily apparent from careful examination of the institution's financial reports. A shareholder or registered representative must have, at a minimum, fundamental knowledge of accounting terms, procedures, and analysis in order to interpret such data competently. This chapter presents and identifies *basic* information in plain English. We may depart from the jargon and techniques used by professional accountants and securities analysts, but the end results will be similar, if not identical.

After studying this chapter, you will understand the construction and analysis of three corporate financial statements. You should be able to do the following:

1. List the three main parts of a balance sheet and their subdivisions
2. Analyze a balance sheet by computing at least four ratios related to book value and capitalization
3. Trace the effects of typical corporate events upon a balance sheet
4. List the main elements of an income statement
5. Analyze an income statement by computing at least five different ratios related to earning power

What Is a Balance Sheet?

Periodically, a corporation needs to demonstrate to its shareholders what the company is worth. The company simply lists the historic cost of everything it owns (assets) and everything it owes (liabilities). *Assets* are items of value—things that a company *owns* or has *owed to it*. Assets are a corporation's possessions, or its pluses. *Liabilities* are the company's obligations—its debts, or what the company *owes*. The difference between assets and liabilities represents the company's net worth or the stockholders' net ownership, called *stockholders' equity*. This tabulation of assets, liabilities, and net worth is known as a *balance sheet*. Traditionally, the balance sheet is arranged as follows:

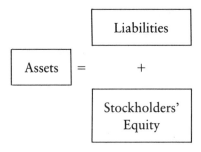

The sides of the equation "balance" because a corporation's stockholders have a stake in their corporation equal to the amount by which the corporation's assets *exceed* its liabilities. Expressed another way, what a company owns (assets) minus what it owes (liabilities) is equal to its net worth. The net worth (stockholders' equity) represents the historic-cost-based value of the shareholders' investment in the corporation. It is the amount of money invested in the business by stockholders, plus the profits that have *not* been paid out as dividends. The basic balance sheet equation is

Total assets = Total liabilities + Stockholders' equity

Since the company's financial state is continually changing, the balance sheet must be dated. The balance sheet's date indicates on which day the tabulations were made. The assets, liabilities, and stockholders' equity are listed at their values *at the close of business* on the date shown at the top of the statement. A *simplified* balance sheet for Roxbury Manufacturing Company appears in Figure 4.1.

The historic cost or book value of the items owned—the assets—can be figured many different ways. In actuality, the amount of money received from buyers, should all the assets be sold (liquidated), differs dramatically from the book values shown on the balance sheet. The shareholders' (stockholders') equity therefore represents the amount of money that *would* go to the preferred and common stockholders if all the company's assets were sold at the book value carried on the balance sheet and if all liabilities were paid. In another form then, the balance sheet equation is

Shareholders' equity = Total assets – Total liabilities

FIGURE 4.1   Typical Balance Sheet

BALANCE SHEET

ROXBURY MANUFACTURING COMPANY
December 31, 1988

	Liabilities	
Accounts payable		$200,000
Accrued expenses		150,000
Accrued taxes		50,000
Total current liabilities		$400,000
Convertible debentures— 8% interest, due 1995		500,000
Total liabilities		$900,000

	Assets	
Cash	$	75,000
Marketable securities		150,000
Accounts receivable		375,000
Inventory		400,000
Total current assets		$1,000,000
Property, plant, and equipment	$	605,000
Prepayments		20,000
Intangibles		10,000
Total assets		$1,635,000

=   +

	Stockholders' Equity	
Preferred stock—6% cumulative ($100 par) authorized, issued, and outstanding 750 shares		$ 75,000
Common stock ($10 par)		300,000
Capital surplus		100,000
Retained earnings		260,000
Total stockholders' equity		$735,000
Total liabilities and stockholders' equity		$1,635,000

Balance Sheet Construction

Let us "build" a sample balance sheet for a typical manufacturing corporation, a block at a time, explaining each item separately.

$$\boxed{\text{ASSETS}}$$

A corporation's assets are traditionally listed, by type, in the following order:

1. *Current* assets
2. *Fixed* assets
3. *Other* assets
4. *Intangibles*

Current Assets

Current assets are items that a company owns or has owed to it, which, in the normal course of business, will be converted into cash within a year or less. This category includes cash, marketable securities, accounts receivable, and inventory.

Cash

In addition to bank deposits, cash consists of the bills and coins in the corporate "till." Bank deposits are usually of the demand type, such as *checking* account balances.

Marketable Securities

Companies invest cash that is not needed immediately, usually in short-term instruments such as Treasury bills. The value of such investments is shown on the balance sheet at the *lower* cost or market value. In the vast majority of cases the market value of the securities is higher than their cost, so *cost* usually appears on the balance sheet. An indication elsewhere, possibly in a footnote, cites the current market value of the securities.

Accounts Receivable

Most manufacturing companies sell to wholesalers or distributors. Goods are usually shipped with payment expected within 15 to 90 days depending on the firm's policies. The total amount of billings outstanding represents the amount of money due the company for goods already shipped. Since the *entire* amount of the billings will probably not be collected for various reasons (for example, bankruptcy of the buyer), an estimate of bad debts is made. This *allowance for bad debt* is deducted from the total accounts receivable so that only the amount that is expected to be collected is shown on the balance sheet.

Inventory

Inventory includes raw materials (the cost of materials to be used to produce products), work in progress (the cost of partially completed products including raw materials, factory labor, and manufacturing overhead), and finished goods (the cost of products ready for sale). Like marketable securities, inventories are carried on the balance sheet at the lower of cost or market value. Usually, the market value of the inventory is higher than its cost: A manufacturing corporation make its profit by selling its finished goods for more than it costs to produce them. Cost accounting for inventory is based on two popular methods: FIFO (first-in/first-out) and LIFO (last-in/first-out). The method that a company chooses can have a dramatic effect on its earnings and on the value of the inventory remaining after a sale.

EXAMPLE

Our example company, Roxbury Manufacturing, has three manufactured inventory items in inventory, each one produced in successive months at successively higher costs. During inflationary periods, such a situation is the norm. The first item manufactured (the one longest in inventory) cost $100. The second item cost $110, and the last item cost $120. The company is now selling its products for $300 each. The selling price less the cost of the product sold is called *gross profit*. Under FIFO the gross profit is $200, since the item sold is assumed to be the first item produced at a cost of $100. The value of the inventory remaining after the sale totals $230 ($110 + $120). Under the LIFO method, the profit on $300 is based on the last item produced (at a cost of $120), and the gross profit is therefore only $180. The remaining inventory valuation is $210 ($100 + $110).

During inflationary periods (for the firm), therefore, the FIFO method yields higher profits (and higher taxes) than LIFO. FIFO also results in higher inventory valuation on the balance sheet. During *deflationary* periods, the results are just the opposite on the balance sheet. Figure 4.2 provides a visual aid to help you remember the effects of LIFO over FIFO during inflationary periods.

Total Current Assets

The sum of these four types of current assets is the corporation's *total current assets*. Now more detail can be added to the current asset portion of the sample balance sheet in Figure 4.1. Compare the section below with the first section in that figure.[2]

Current Assets	
Cash	$ 75,000
Marketable securities at cost	
(Market value – $156,000)	150,000
Accounts receivable ($390,000 less $15,000 allowance for bad debt)	375,000
Inventory (first-in/first-out)	400,000
Total current assets	$1,000,000

Current assets are converted into cash, and cash is converted into other current assets continuously. When a company sells its products, an appropriate amount is deducted from inventory and is recorded in accounts receivable. When buyers pay their bills, accounts receivable become cash, and the cash may then be used to pay debts. A company also may add to inventory and thereby repeat the cycle.

[2]Some corporate balance sheets may show additional items such as notes receivable and/or prepaid expenses. Prepaid expenses will be discussed later on in this chapter since the bookkeeping method we have chosen treats prepaid expenses as another asset rather than as a current asset. This variation is just one example of the methods used by modern accountants.

FIGURE 4.2   **Inventory Cost Accounting**

LIFO = Lower gross profits
Lower taxes
Lower inventory valuation

3 ITEMS IN INVENTORY LISTED AT COST

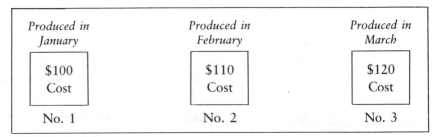

Produced in January	*Produced in February*	*Produced in March*
$100 Cost	$110 Cost	$120 Cost
No. 1	No. 2	No. 3

FIFO

Under FIFO (first-in/first-out), item No. 1—the *first* one produced—is paired against the sale at $300. Thus:

$100 Cost   Sold at ⟶ $300   = $200 gross profit

No. 1

This leaves $110 Cost   + $120 Cost   = $230 value of remaining inventory

No. 2   No. 3

LIFO

Under LIFO (last-in/first-out), item No. 3—the *last* one produced—is paired against the sale at $300. Thus:

$120 Cost   Sold at ⟶ $300   = $180 gross profit

No. 3

This leaves $100 Cost   + $110 Cost   = $210 value of remaining inventory

No. 1   No. 2

Current assets are typically listed in order of liquidity with the most liquid current asset (cash) listed first. Cash, marketable securities, accounts receivable, and finally inventory is the appropriate order for the current assets we have considered here.

Quick Assets

Current assets that may be *quickly* converted into cash, should the company decide it is necessary, are called *quick assets*. The only item under current assets that is *not* considered very liquid is inventory. Therefore, to calculate *quick assets,* subtract inventory from total current assets.

Let's review current assets.

QUESTIONS

1. Prepare the current assets portion of a corporation's balance sheet using the following information:

Inventory—market value	$2,932,000
Inventory—cost	1,400,000
Cash on hand	58,000
Checking account balance	204,000
Accounts receivable	1,140,000
Provision for returns and uncollectables	47,000
Marketable securities—cost	375,000
Marketable securities—market value	389,000

2. What are this corporation's quick assets?

ANSWERS

1.

Cash	$ 262,000
Marketable securities at cost	
(Market value = $389,000)	375,000
Accounts receivable	
(Allowance for bad debt = $47,000)	1,093,000
Inventory	1,400,000
Total current assets	$3,130,000

Note that the listing for cash includes the value of both cash and checking account balances: $58,000 + $204,000 = $262,000. The marketable securities are shown at the *lower* of cost or market; they are therefore listed at $375,000 rather than $389,000. Accounts receivable are shown *after* subtracting the provision for returns and uncollectables (bad debt provision): $1,140,000 − $47,000 = $1,093,000. The inventory must be shown at the lower of cost or market value; therefore, it is listed at $1,400,000 rather than $2,932,000.

2. $1,730,000

Quick assets are equal to total current assets less inventory:

$3,130,000 − $1,400,000 = $1,730,000

They are also equal to the sum of cash, marketable securities, and accounts receivable:

$262,000 + $375,000 + $1,093,000 = $1,730,000

EXAMPLE

Cash	$ 75,000
Marketable securities	150,000
Accounts receivable	375,000
Inventory	400,000
Total current assets	$1,000,000

Subtracting inventory ($400,000) from the total ($1,000,000), we arrive at a figure of $600,000 for quick assets. Of course, the same amount may be derived by adding together cash, marketable securities, and accounts receivable. The formulas are as follows:

$$\boxed{\text{Quick assets} = \text{Total current assets} - \text{Inventory}}$$

$$\text{Quick assets} = \$1,000,000 - \$400,000$$
$$= \$600,000$$

or

$$\boxed{\text{Quick assets} = \begin{array}{c} \text{Cash} + \text{Marketable securities} \\ + \text{ Accounts receivable} \end{array}}$$

$$\text{Quick assets} = \$75,000 + \$150,000 + \$375,000$$
$$= \$600,000$$

Current Liabilities

Now refer to the *other* (right) side of the balance sheet of our example company to examine the debts of the corporation that are scheduled for payment within one year. This quick comparison determines in a shorthand way (as accountants do) whether enough money is available to stay in business during the short run, say, the next year. Since current assets, at least in theory, represent the source from which current liabilities are paid, we need to know how the current debts compare with the current (or possibly the quick) assets.

Current liabilities typically include the following items:

Accounts payable, the amount the company owes to its business creditors

Accrued expenses, amounts owed to its salespeople in salaries and wages, interest on debt, and all other unpaid items

Accrued taxes, federal, state, and local taxes owed, Social Security (FICA) deductions, and local government levies withheld from employees

Notes payable, monies owed to banks, to other lenders, or on outstanding bonds that are due to be paid within the year

The current liabilities section of the balance sheet of our typical manufacturing corporation is as follows:

Accounts payable	$200,000
Accrued expenses	150,000
Accrued taxes	+ 50,000
Total current liabilities	$400,000

Relating Current Assets to Current Liabilities

Working Capital

The relationship between current assets and current liabilities is important. After all, it is certainly necessary for a corporation to be able to pay its obligations when they become due. Most firms have more current assets than current liabilities. The difference between current assets and current liabilities is called *working capital*. It represents the amount of money that would be left from the current assets if all current assets were converted into cash and all current liabilities were paid. This important figure is derived by using the following formula:

$$\text{Working capital} = \text{Current assets} - \text{Current liabilities}$$

A company's ability to meet its short-term obligations is measured, at least in part, by the amount of its working capital. Working capital is also known as *net working capital* or *net current assets*.

EXAMPLE

Assets		*Liabilities*	
Cash	$75,000	Accounts payable	$200,000
+Marketable securities	150,000	+Accrued expenses	150,000
+Accounts receivable	375,000	+Accrued taxes	50,000
+Inventory	400,000		
Total current assets	$1,000,000	Total current liabilities	$400,000

For our corporation:

$$
\begin{aligned}
\text{Working capital} &= \text{Current assets} - \text{Current liabilities} \\
&= \$1,000,000 - \$400,000 \\
&= \$600,000
\end{aligned}
$$

Current Ratio

A *dollar* figure for working capital is difficult to interpret, especially when comparing companies. A company may have only a modest amount of current liabilities, requiring a relatively small amount of working capital, or its current liabilities may be very large, requiring many more dollars of working capital as a safety margin. Of primary importance, therefore, is the *proportion* by which current assets exceed current liabilities. This ratio, called the *current ratio*, is calculated by dividing current assets by current liabilities. Therefore:

$$\text{Current ratio} = \frac{\text{Current assets}}{\text{Current liabilities}}$$

Using the figures from our example:

$$\text{Current ratio} = \frac{\$1,000,000}{\$400,000} = 2.5$$

A current ratio equal to 2.5 indicates that our typical corporation can cover its current liabilities by more than 2½ times. In other words, for every *dollar* of current liabilities, it has *2.5 dollars* of current assets.

There is no "ideal" value for the current ratio. If a firm's current ratio is too low (for example, zero), then it is unlikely that the firm will be able to meet its short-term obligations. However, a very large current ratio (for example, 100) indicates that the firm is not using its assets wisely since most current assets are not productive and do not produce profits for the company. Further, a firm may choose to have a low current ratio minimizing its unproductive assets or have a large line of credit with a financial institution as a substitute for liquidity.

It is important to compare the current ratio of the company to those of similar companies. Industry statistics are available for most financial ratios of this type. Some industries (for example, utilities) typically have low current ratios (1.0) because their cash flows are easy to predict. Manufacturing companies typically have current ratios of about 2.0.

Quick Asset Ratio

A more stringent test of a company's ability to meet its current obligations is the *quick asset ratio,* also called the *acid test ratio.* This ratio indicates the relationship between *quick assets* and current liabilities:

$$\text{Quick asset ratio} = \frac{\text{Quick assets}}{\text{Current liabilities}}$$

EXAMPLE

Using the figures for our example company:

$$\text{Quick assets} = \text{Total current assets} - \text{Inventory}$$

$$\text{Quick assets} = \$1,000,000 - \$400,000$$
$$= \$600,000$$

$$\text{Quick asset ratio} = \frac{\text{Quick assets}}{\text{Total current liabilities}}$$

$$\text{Quick asset ratio} = \frac{\$600,000}{\$400,000} = 1.5$$

The quick asset ratio of 1.5 indicates that our corporation had one and one-half times the total of its short-term liabilities in quick assets alone. A typical quick asset ratio for a manufacturing concern is 1 to 1. In other words, the corporation should have enough *quick* assets to pay off *all* the current liabilities.

Let's review.

QUESTIONS

Answer the questions below using the following information.

Current Assets		Current Liabilities	
Cash	$50,000	Accounts payable	$ 80,000
Securities	5,000	Accrued expenses	75,000
Accounts receivable	165,000	Dividends payable	10,000
Inventory	280,000	Current maturities of long-term debt	75,000
	$500,000		$240,000

1. What is the corporation's working capital? *CA – CL*

2. What is the corporation's current ratio? $\frac{CA}{CL}$

3. Based on the information provided, is the current ratio adequate? *Yes*

4. What is the corporation's quick asset ratio? $\frac{QA}{CL}$ *QA = CA – I* $\frac{220,000}{240,00}$

5. Based on the criteria given, is the quick asset ratio adequate? *No*

ANSWERS

1. $260,000

Working capital = Current assets – Current liabilities
$260,000 = $500,000 – $240,000

2. | 2.08 to 1 |

$$\text{Current ratio} = \frac{\text{Current assets}}{\text{Current liabilities}}$$

$$= \frac{\$500{,}000}{\$240{,}000} = 2.08, \text{ or } 2.1, \text{ or approximately 2 to 1}$$

3. | Yes | Current ratio of 2 or better is considered adequate.

4. | 0.92 to 1 |

$$\text{Liquidity ratio} = \frac{\text{Quick assets}}{\text{Current liabilities}}$$

$$= \frac{\$220{,}000}{\$240{,}000} = 0.92$$

5. | No |

An adequate liquidity ratio is considered to be 1 or better. If it isn't this high, the company may have difficulty obtaining funds to pay off its $75,000 long-term maturing debt.

Fixed Assets

Now that we have considered both current assets and current liabilities, let us turn our attention to the remainder of the left-hand (asset) side of the balance sheet.

Items of value used in a firm's operations that are expected to generate revenue are referred to as *fixed assets*. Included in this category are such items as land, buildings, furniture and fixtures, machinery, tools, and transportation equipment—sometimes referred to collectively as *property, plant, and equipment*. These assets are usually not considered as items to be sold but rather as "tools of the trade" with which the manufactured product is produced, displayed, and transported. Most fixed assets are listed on the balance sheet at *cost minus accumulated depreciation.* However, certain items such as land are not depreciated. For our typical manufacturing corporation, the fixed assets are $605,000, as shown on the balance sheet under property, plant, and equipment. (See Figure 4.1.)

Depreciation

As most fixed assets age, they decrease in value due to ordinary wear and tear, action of the elements, or obsolescence. When a fixed asset is acquired by the corporation it is *not* charged as a business expense immediately. Since a fixed asset is expected to be useful for more than 1 year, the company charges it as an expense, *a little bit at a time,* spread over the years it is expected to be usable to the company. By way of analogy, assume you as an individual (were it legal) could *spread out* a deductible personal expense of $5,000 for a car. Instead of taking the full $5,000 deduction in the year in which you incurred the actual expense, you could instead deduct $1,000 a year for 5 consecutive years, thus *spreading out* the expense. Spreading out the expense is not only legal but mandatory for the corporation. Corporations can deduct depreciation in various ways. The amount by which the fixed assets are lowered each year is the portion of the cost of fixed assets charged as an expense for a given year; that portion is called *annual depreciation* and is listed as such on the income statement. The sum of all depreciation expense on a firm's fixed assets is shown as accumulated depreciation on the balance sheet.

Three Methods for Determining Amount of Depreciation

Fixed assets may be depreciated by numerous methods. Three principal methods are

1. Straight-line
2. Sum-of-years' digits
3. Double-declining balance

When a fixed asset is purchased, the company estimates how long the asset is expected to be used *(useful life).* It also estimates the value that it expects to receive when the asset is scrapped *(salvage value)*. The depreciable cost of the asset is considered to be the initial price *minus* the salvage value because the salvage value will be received some time after the item is purchased. In most cases, this net cost figure is the amount depreciated over the item's useful life. The simple equation is as follows:

$$\text{Depreciable cost} = \text{Actual cost} - \text{Salvage value}$$

(A practice that is accepted by the Internal Revenue Service is to ignore any salvage value of less than 10 percent because depreciation and salvage value are estimates. In our examples, we *will* always use salvage values.)

In each of the following examples for determining the amount of depreciation, the fixed asset is purchased for $40,000. It is expected to have a useful life of 5 years and a salvage value of $10,000.

$$\begin{aligned}
\text{Depreciable cost} &= \text{Actual cost} - \text{Salvage value} \\
&= \$40,000 - \$10,000 \\
&= \$30,000
\end{aligned}$$

STRAIGHT-LINE DEPRECIATION.   Straight-line depreciation is the simplest and most used method. To determine the amount of each year's depreciation, divide the depreciable cost of the item (actual cost − salvage value) by the number of years of useful life.

$$\text{Annual depreciation} = \frac{\text{Depreciable cost}}{\text{Years of useful life}}$$

$$\text{Annual depreciation} = \frac{\$30,000}{5} = \$6,000$$

Fixed assets are carried at *cost less accumulated depreciation*. At the end of the items' first year of use, the fixed asset section of the balance sheet shows:

Fixed Assets

Cost	$40,000
Accumulated depreciation	− 6,000
	$34,000

The annual write-off (depreciation) is the same in years 2 through 5. At the end of the second year, the *accumulated* depreciation is $12,000 ($6,000 from year 1 *plus* $6,000 from year 2), and the balance sheet shows:

Fixed Assets

Cost	$40,000
Accumulated depreciation	− 12,000
	$28,000

By year 5, accumulated depreciation totals $30,000, and the asset has been "written down" to a carrying value of $10,000, its salvage value. The total picture in chart form is shown in Figure 4.3.

Sum-of-years' digits depreciation.   To find each year's depreciation, write down the number of expected years of useful life (5, in this example) and "count down" to 1, adding the years' digits as you go:

FIGURE 4.3   Straight-Line Method

Year		Annual Depreciation	Accumulated Depreciation	Asset's Balance Sheet Value
1	$30,000 ÷ 5 =	$6,000	$ 6,000	$34,000
2	30,000 ÷ 5 =	6,000	12,000	28,000
3	30,000 ÷ 5 =	6,000	18,000	22,000
4	30,000 ÷ 5 =	6,000	24,000	16,000
5	30,000 ÷ 5 =	6,000	30,000	10,000

Note that each year's depreciation is 20 percent of the net cost of the fixed assets since we are working with a useful life of 5 years (100% − 5 = 20%).

$$5 + 4 + 3 + 2 + 1$$

Adding the numbers together, you get 15. For each year, use the first number in your "count down" sequence as the numerator and the *total* number (15) as the denominator. Thus for year 1:

$$\text{Annual depreciation} = \frac{\text{Useful life}}{\text{Sum of years' digits}} \times \text{Net cost}$$

$$\text{Annual depreciation} = \frac{5}{15} \times \$30,000$$

$$= \$10,000$$

Use this same procedure for each subsequent year, taking the next lower number in sequence as the numerator and the total of all digits as the denominator. The 5-year effect is shown in Figure 4.4.

FIGURE 4.4   Sum-of-Years' Digits Method

Year		Annual Depreciation	Accumulated Depreciation	Asset's Balance Sheet Value
1	$\frac{5}{15} \times \$30,000 =$	$10,000	$10,000	$30,000
2	$\frac{4}{15} \times 30,000 =$	8,000	18,000	22,000
3	$\frac{3}{15} \times 30,000 =$	6,000	24,000	16,000
4	$\frac{2}{15} \times 30,000 =$	4,000	28,000	12,000
5	$\frac{1}{15} \times 30,000 =$	2,000	30,000	10,000

Figure 4.4 shows that at the end of the first year, the balance is:

Fixed Assets

Cost	$40,000	
Accumulated depreciation	− 10,000	
		$30,000

The balance at the end of the *second year* is:

Cost	$40,000	
Accumulated depreciation	− 18,000	
		$22,000

The sum-of-years' digits is a method of *accelerated depreciation.* More depreciation is charged off in the *early* years of the assets useful life and less in *later* years. Compared with the straight-line method, the sum-of-years' digits method causes earnings in the first few years to be *lower* and earnings in later years to be *higher.* Lower *earnings* also means lower *taxes,* at least in the early years of the asset's life.

DOUBLE-DECLINING-BALANCE DEPRECIATION. Double-declining-balance depreciation is a method of accelerated depreciation that also affords relatively large write-offs for depreciation in the early years of the fixed asset's life. Yet it differs from other methods in two significant ways.

1. The net book value of the asset is used, *not* the depreciable cost: that is, salvage value is *not* subtracted from the actual cost.
2. As with all depreciation methods, the book value of a fixed asset is never decreased below the expected salvage value. However, special attention must be paid to this rule when using the double-declining-balance method because of the nature of the calculations.

These differences are not as radical as they might first appear. In the straight-line and sum-of-years' digits methods, the asset is written down from its depreciable cost to zero ($40,000 − $10,000 to zero) for a total write-off of $30,000. Under the double-declining-balance method, the asset is written down from its initial book value or acquisition cost to its salvage value ($40,000 to $10,000), *still* adding up to a total write-off of $30,000.

To figure each year's write-off with this method, *double* what it would be under the straight-line method. Since the annual depreciation is 20 percent (in our 5-year life example) for straight-line, then it is 40 percent for double-declining balance. An alternate way of arriving at this percentage is to divide 2 by the number of years of useful life: $2 \div 5 = 0.40$, or a 40 percent annual write-off.

Year 1: 40% of $40,000 = $16,000 annual depreciation

Obviously we cannot continue to write off 40 percent of an asset's value each year for the full 5 years. So in all years subsequent to the first, we write off 40 percent of the *remaining* book value of the asset—or 40 percent of the "declining balance" of the book value. (See Figure 4.5.) The total amount of depreciation taken over the life of the asset is never more than its depreciable value, and the asset's balance sheet value is *not* written down below its salvage value. Although the actual treatment of the write-off after year 2 is beyond the scope of this chapter, the general approach and effect of this method is apparent.

FIGURE 4.5   Declining-Balance Method for 2 Years Only

Year			Annual Depreciation	Accumulated Depreciation	Asset's Balance Sheet Value
1	40% of $40,000	=	$16,000	$16,000	$24,000
2	40% of $40,000	=	9,600	25,600	14,400

Comparing the Three Methods for Determining Depreciation

The effect on the income statement and balance sheet of each method for calculating annual depreciation is different. With the straight-line method, costs are evened out over the expected useful life of the asset, and a high remaining value is listed for the asset in the later years. With the sum-of-years' digits method and the double-declining-balance method, a large write-off is taken in the early years, thereby lowering early profits as well as early taxes. With both methods, a lower remaining value is listed in the later years. Since the double-declining-balance method *accelerates* depreciation the most, it is used when the chief concern is to lower taxes in the early years of an asset's useful life.

It is permissible to use one method of depreciation for reporting to stockholders and another for purposes of filing a tax return. Very often a company reports to its stockholders on a *straight-line basis* and files its tax return on a method similar to the *double-declining-balance method*, since this produces a higher expense and, subsequently, a lower tax. Currently, tax laws allow either straight-line depreciation or the accelerated cost recovery system method. Tax laws, however, are beyond the scope of this book and will not be discussed here.

Test your knowledge of depreciation methods.

QUESTIONS

1. A company purchases a new machine tool for $60,000. The tool is expected to have a useful life of 10 years and a salvage value of $5,000.
   a. What is the annual depreciation for the first 3 years of the asset's useful life using the straight-line depreciation method?
   b. How will the asset be listed on the balance sheet at the end of the third year using the straight-line depreciation method?

2. Using the figures in question 1, calculate the answers to a and b under the sum-of-years' digits method.

3. Use the figures in question 1 to calculate a and b using the double-declining-balance method.
4. Under which of the three methods will the company pay less income tax during the *first* 3 years?

ANSWERS

1. *Straight-line (SL)*

$$\text{Annual write-off} = (\text{Cost} - \text{Salvage value}) \div \frac{\text{Number of years}}{\text{of useful life}}$$

$$\text{Annual write-off} = (\$60,000 - \$5,000) \div 10 = \$5,500$$

a.

Year	Annual Depreciation
1	$5,500
2	$5,500
3	$5,500

b. $43,500

The accumulated depreciation by the end of the third year is $16,500 ($5,500 + $5,500 + $5,500). This amount is deducted from the asset's cost, and the difference is the amount at which the asset is carried on the balance sheet (its *book value*).

$$\begin{array}{l}\text{Book value} \\ \text{(at end of year 3)}\end{array} = \text{Cost} - \text{Accumulated depreciation}$$

$$\begin{array}{l}\text{Book value} \\ \text{(at end of year 3)}\end{array} = \$60,000 - \$16,500 = \$43,500$$

2. *Sum-of-years' digits (SOYD)*
Add the years of useful life, last year first:

$$10 + 9 + 8 + 7 + 6 + 5 + 4 + 3 + 2 + 1 = 55$$

Use the first number in the sequence as the numerator and the *total* number as the denominator for the first year—and so on for each subsequent year. Multiply this fraction by the asset's depreciative cost (actual cost − salvage value).

a.

Year			Annual Depreciation
1	$= \dfrac{10}{55}$ × \$55,000 =		\$10,000
2	$= \dfrac{9}{55}$ × 55,000 =		9,000
3	$= \dfrac{8}{55}$ × 55,000 =		8,000

b. $33,000

The accumulated depreciation by the of the third year is $27,000 ($10,000 + $9,000 + $8,000). This amount is deducted from the asset's cost to arrive at the "book value" at the end of the third year.

$$\text{Book value (at end of year 3)} = \text{Cost} - \text{Accumulated depreciation}$$

$$\text{Book value (at end of year 3)} = \$60,000 - \$27,000 = \$33,000$$

3. *Double-declining balance (DDB)*
   Each year's write-off is made at *double* the straight-line rate. With the straight-line method, the write-off is 10 percent. Therefore, the double-declining-balance rate is 20 percent. The alternate method is to divide 2 by the number of years of useful life:

   $$\frac{2}{10} = 0.20, \text{ or } 20\%$$

   Remember that each subsequent year's write-off is 20 percent of the *remaining* value of the asset's declining balance after the previous year's write-off. Use the *full* actual cost of the asset, not *depreciable* cost.

a.

Year		Annual Depreciation	Asset's Remaining Value
1	20% of $60,000 =	$12,000	$48,000
2	20% of $48,000 =	9,600	38,400
3	20% of $38,400 =	7,680	30,720

b. $30,720

   The accumulated depreciation at the end of the third year is $29,280 ($12,000 + $9,600 + $7,680). This amount is deducted from the actual cost to arrive at the remaining book value.

   Book value   = Cost − Accumulated depreciation
   (at end of year 3)
   Book value   = $60,000 − $29,280 = $30,720
   (at end of year 3)

4. | *Double-declining balance*

During the first 3 years, the company writes off more than $29,000 toward depreciation. This "deductible" amount affords greater tax savings in the early years than the $27,000 from the sum-of-years' digits method or the $16,500 from the straight-line method.

The company, in effect, shows greater "expenses" by this method. Therefore, it reports smaller income and pays less tax.

In the *later* years of the asset's useful life, the tables turn, and both accelerated methods (SOYD and DDB) show *smaller* depreciation than straight line.

Other Assets

Other assets is a *miscellaneous* category that generally includes prepaid expenses, deferred charges, and other items that are usually considered investments for the future. *Prepaid expenses* include payments for materials or services in *advance* of their receipt or use such as early rent payments and insurance premiums. *Deferred charges* are used to "charge off" major expenses such as those incurred in the introduction of a new product or the formation of a new subsidiary company.

EXAMPLE

A company spends $1,000,000 to purchase a 10-year lease in a given year. It records $100,000 as an expense for the first year and includes $900,000 in the other assets section so that the *total assets* section shows a decline of only $100,000 for the year. The company considers $900,000 of the total amount spent as an asset in terms of having a lease. The balance sheet shows cash minus $1,000,000 and other assets plus $900,000. The company can reduce the $900,000 in each subsequent year for the next 9 years so that it spreads out the $1,000,000 cost for the lease over a *10-year period*.

Intangible Assets

Included in the intangible assets category are items of value that have no physical existence, such as patents, franchises, and goodwill. Such items are very difficult to quantify. Traditionally, intangibles are the last item shown on the asset side of the balance sheet. Most of these assets are expensed (amortized) using a straight-line method.

╔═══════════════╗
║   LIABILITIES   ║
╚═══════════════╝

Liabilities

Let us turn our attention again to the *right* side (liabilities) of the balance sheet. The corporation's debts and, further down, the stockholders' equity are listed here.

Current Liabilities

The first category, *current liabilities*, includes all obligations that must be paid (mature) within the year. (Refer to the section "Current Liabilities" for a complete description.)

Noncurrent Liabilities

The *noncurrent liabilities* appear below current liabilities on the balance sheet. Usually, the major item is the corporation's funded debt, in many cases outstanding bonds maturing one year or more in the future. This category may also include long-term promissory notes, bank loans, and other corporate obligations.

Bonds are carried on the balance sheet at the price at which they are initially issued. Keep in mind that the actual market prices of the company's own bonds *could* be either at a premium (above par) or at a discount (below par). The coupon rate and maturity date are usually indicated for each outstanding bond. The liabilities section of the balance sheet for our typical manufacturing corporation looks like this:

Liabilities

Accounts payable	$200,000	
Accrued expenses	150,000	
Accrued taxes	+ 50,000	
Total current liabilities		$400,000
Convertible debentures 8% interest, due 1995		+ 500,000
Total liabilities		$900,000

> SHAREHOLDERS' EQUITY

Stockholders' (Shareholders') Equity

The difference between the corporations' total assets and total liabilities is referred to as *stockholders' equity* or net worth. The last section of the balance sheet represents the stockholders' equity, which is the book (or accounting) value of the stake that the stockholders (both common and preferred) have in their corporation. This section itemizes the amount of equity or *ownership* of the owners of the corporation—the shareholders. The following items are commonly found in this category:

1. Preferred stock
2. Common stock
3. Paid-in capital (capital surplus)
4. Retained earnings (earned surplus)
5. Treasury stock

Preferred Stock

Preferred stock, like common stock, is an equity security. Holders of such stock are considered to be owners of the corporation. By contrast, bondholders are considered creditors. Fittingly, preferred stock, which is ordinarily senior to common stock with respect to dividends and liquidation rights, is listed first. Such stock is "carried" *not* at its market value, but at the value at which it was initially issued, which in most cases is approximately equal to its total par value. This listed figure approximates the amount that the preferred shareholders are entitled to receive should the company be dissolved.

Most balance sheets detail information about preferred stock listings, such as par value, convertibility (if any), dividend rate, and the number of authorized shares, issued shares, and outstanding shares.

EXAMPLE

Preferred stock $75,000

6% Cumulative—$100 par
Authorized, issued, and outstanding
750 shares

(*Note:* All 750 authorized shares of preferred stock are issued and outstanding.)

750 Shares × $100 Par = $75,000 Book value (Total par value)

Each share of $100 par preferred stock is entitled to a dividend at 6 percent of the par value each year. In other words, 6 percent of $100 equals a $6-per-share annual dividend. The balance sheet indicates that such dividends are cumulative. In the event that any preferred dividends are "skipped," the company may not pay dividends to the common stockholders until all back dividends on the preferred stock (arrearages) have been paid.

Common Stock

The balance sheet shows the number of shares of common stock outstanding and their par value. Historically, par value represented the minimum price at which the shares could be sold by the corporation. After the initial offering, par value has very little real significance. For our purposes, let's consider the amount shown on the balance sheet as "common stock" to represent the company's "seed money"—the amount of money, *at par value,* that the company first received from the sale of stock. In recent years, because stock transfer taxes are based on par values, corporations are assigning par value well *below* the price at which the shares are sold. Today, par value has little or no meaning in terms of the actual share value.

EXAMPLE

Common stock $300,000

$10 par
Authorized, issued, and outstanding 30,000 shares

Paid-in Capital

Paid-in capital, also called *capital surplus,* shows the amount of money the company received from the sale of shares of common stock to the public *in addition* to the par value.

EXAMPLE

Roxbury Manufacturing starts in business by selling 20,000 shares of stock at original par value of $10 per share. After this initial offering, the common stock section of the balance sheet shows $200,000. At least at this point in time, there is no *paid-in* capital. If, at a later date, the company issues another 10,000 shares at *$20* each, the "extra" monies received—*over* par value—are indicated in the paid-in capital section of the balance sheet. The *basic* amount received ($10 par value) is added to the common stock account. The overage (the $10 that *exceeded* par value) is placed into the paid-in capital account.

Common stock $300,000

$10 par
Authorized, issued and outstanding 30,000 shares

Paid-in capital (capital surplus)   100,000

This entry indicates that the owners of the business invested a total of $400,000 in common stock, of which $100,000 exceeded the total par value of $300,000. Generally, therefore, the *total* of these two accounts (common stock and paid-in capital) indicates the amount of money the company has received through the sale of its common stock to investors.

Treasury Stock

Treasury stock is the firm's stock that it repurchases from shareholders. It is shown on the balance sheet as a reduction of shareholders' equity. The value of the treasury stock on the balance sheet is equal to the amount that was paid for the stock. If treasury stock is "resold" to shareholders, the treasury stock is reduced by the amount paid to repurchase the shares, and any excess or deficit is recorded in the paid-in capital account.

Retained Earnings

Also know as *earned surplus,* the retained earnings account shows the amount of profit that the company has retained in the business *after* paying all dividends on the common and preferred stocks. In a sense, retained earnings represent profits that have not yet been paid out to the stockholders in the form of dividends.

EXAMPLE

A company is formed by selling a share of common stock at $100 per share to 10 different people. The total amount collected is used to purchase goods at wholesale—for subsequent resale. An early balance sheet is as follows:

Assets		*Liabilities*	
Inventory	$1,000		-0-

	Stockholders' Equity	
Common stock	$1,000
$100 par	

At this point, total assets ($1,000 in inventory) equal total liabilities (zero) plus stockholders' equity ($1,000). The company decides to sell the inventory for a total of $2,000 and uses all the cash to purchase more inventory. The revised situation is:

	Assets		*Liabilities*	
Inventory	$1,000		-0-	

	Stockholders' Equity
Common stock	$1,000
$100 par	
Retained earnings	$1,000

The $1,000 earned profit, over and above the company's initial investment, appears in the retained earnings account.

The total of $2,000 under stockholders' equity, however, does not mean that the shareholders will receive a $20 return for their $10 investments. These retained earnings are *not* cash. The profit has already been reinvested in additional inventory. Since the average balance sheet lists many items at *other than* their liquidation values, the chances of the shareholders' receiving cash equal to the net worth (shareholders' equity) portion of the balance sheet are small. Remember that shareholders' equity represents the amount that the stockholders *would* receive *if* all assets were sold at the values at which they are carried on the balance sheet (book value) and *if* all liabilities were paid off at their balance sheet figures.

EXAMPLE

A company is formed through the sale of 1,000 shares of preferred stock at $100 per share and 500,000 shares of common stock at $1 per share. It uses some of the cash received to purchase machinery and raw materials, but it does not pay for all the items in full. Our balance sheet is as follows:

Assets		*Liabilities*	
Cash	$160,000	Accounts payable	$ 50,000
Inventory	+ 85,000		
Total current assets	$245,000	*Stockholders' Equity*	
Property, plant and equipment	+405,000	Preferred stock $100 par	100,000
Total assets	$650,000	Common stock $1 par	+500,000
		Total liabilities and stockholders' equity	$650,000

At this early period of the company's development, it has no profits and therefore no retained earnings. But it operates successfully over time and increases its assets by $200,000 through sales and increases its liabilities by only $50,000. The difference between the value of the newly acquired items and the additional debt—$150,000—represents a "gain" for the company's owners. At least in theory, the stockholders are "worth" $150,000 more, a profit shown as retained earnings. Keep in mind that the $150,000 "earned" is spread out among various assets. To realize this amount in cash, the company would have to liquidate some assets. The balance sheet now looks like this:

Assets		Liabilities	
Cash	$ 80,000	Accounts payable	$ 60,000
Accounts receivable	135,000	Accrued expenses	+ 40,000
Inventory	+140,000	Total liabilities	$100,000
Total current assets	$355,000		
		Stockholders' Equity	
Property, plant, and equipment	470,000	Preferred stock $100 par	100,000
Prepaid expenses	+ 25,000	Common stock $1 par	500,000
Total assets	$850,000	Retained earnings	+150,000
		Total liabilities and stockholders' equity	$850,000

The balance sheet balances. If the company decides to liquidate, it realizes $850,000 in cash from the sale of its assets, at least in *theory*. Next, if it pays off all obligations ($100,000 for all liabilities), it would have a total of $750,000 to be distributed to the owners of the company—its shareholders. The preferred stockholders are entitled to receive par for their stock ($100,000), leaving $650,000 for the common stockholders. The common stockholders' stake in the company can be determined by adding together the common stock listing ($500,000), paid-in capital ($0), and retained earnings ($150,000). The sum of these three figures shows the *common* stockholders' equity.

On the other hand, let us assume the company decides to continue operations for future profits. To reward the stockholders, it decides to distribute a dividend. Since the term *retained earnings* means earnings retained in the business, any distributed earnings in the form of dividends *decrease* the retained earnings.

Balance Sheet Analysis

Now let's analyze the balance sheet by examining capitalization and book value. We have already compared current assets with current liabilities in the section "Relating Current Assets to Current Liabilities." We suggest that you review this section now and consider it as part of the balance sheet analysis.

Capitalization (Capital Structure–Invested Capital)

A company's *capitalization* is the sum of the balance sheet values for the corporation's bonds, preferred stock, and common stock. All *three* elements of the common stock are added: common stock, paid-in capital, and retained earnings. Thus, capitalization represents the monies invested in the company by the *original* purchasers of the bonds, preferred stock, and common stock. It also reflects retained earnings; that is, the capital that has *not* been paid out as dividends but rather has been reinvested in the company. Capitalization indicates how a company acquired its funds.

Capitalization can be expressed in terms of three ratios, one for bonds, common stock, and preferred stock, respectively. Each of these *capitalization ratios* represents the proportion of money collected through each vehicle to the *total* capitalization amount, assuming the total amount is equal to 100 percent.

EXAMPLE

In Figure 4.6, Roxbury's capitalization is shown at $1,235,000, calculated as follows:

$$\text{Bonds} + \frac{\text{Preferred}}{\text{stock}} + \frac{\text{Common}}{\text{stock}} + \frac{\text{Capital}}{\text{surplus}} + \frac{\text{Retained}}{\text{earnings}} = \text{Capitalization}$$

$$\$500,000 + \$75,000 + \$300,000 + \$100,000 + \$260,000 = \$1,235,000$$

FIGURE 4.6   Balance Sheet for Roxbury Manufacturing Company

BALANCE SHEET

ROXBURY MANUFACTURING COMPANY
December 31, 1988

Assets	
Cash	$ 75,000
Marketable securities	150,000
Accounts receivable	375,000
Inventories	+ 400,000
Total current assets	$1,000,000
Property, plant, and equipment	605,000
Prepayments	20,000
Intangibles	10,000
Total assets	$1,635,000

Liabilities	
Accounts payable	$200,000
Accrued expenses	150,000
Accrued taxes	50,000
Total current liabilities	$400,000
Bonds 8%—due 1995	500,000
Total liabilities	$900,000

Stockholders' Equity	
Preferred stock—6% ($100 par)	$ 75,000
Common stock ($10 par)	300,000
Capital surplus *Paid in capital*	100,000
Retained earnings	260,000
Total stockholders' equity	$ 735,000
Total liabilities and stockholders' equity	$1,635,000

The *bond ratio* is derived by dividing total capitalization into the bonded debt, usually those outstanding bonds maturing in 5 years or more.

$$\text{Bond ratio} = \frac{\text{Bonds}}{\text{Total capitalization}}$$

$$\text{Bond ratio} = \frac{\$500,000}{\$1,235,000} = 0.405 \text{ or } 40.5\%$$

The *preferred stock ratio* is found by dividing total capitalization into the par value of the preferred stock.

$$\text{Preferred stock ratio} = \frac{\text{Preferred stock}}{\text{Total capitalization}}$$

$$\text{Preferred stock ratio} = \frac{\$75,000}{\$1,235,000} = 0.061 \text{ or } 6.1\%$$

The *common stock ratio* is found by dividing total capitalization into *all three parts* of the common stock account.

$$\text{Common stock ratio} = \frac{\text{Common stock} + \text{Capital surplus} + \text{Retained earnings}}{\text{Total capitalization}}$$

$$\text{Common stock ratio} = \frac{\$300,000 + \$100,000 + \$260,000}{\$1,235,000} = 0.543 \text{ or } 53.4\%$$

All three capitalization ratios should add up to 100 percent. (See Figure 4.7.)

FIGURE 4.7   Breakdown of Roxbury's Capitalization Ratios

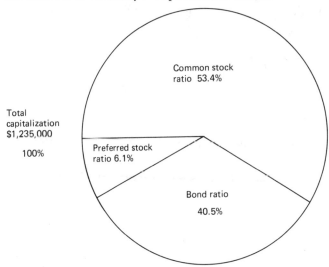

There are several capitalization ratio "yardsticks." For example, if the combined bond and preferred stock ratios exceed 50 percent of the total capitalization, an industrial company is generally considered by industry standards to have a *leveraged* capital structure. This condition may be considered risky.

Book Value

The net tangible assets that back each share of common stock are known as *book value*. Calculating book value is easy. Since the balance sheet always shows the theoretical value of the common stockholders' equity (common stock + paid-in capital + retained earnings), to calculate the book value, subtract the *intangible* assets (if any), and divide by the number of outstanding common shares. The formula, applied to the sample balance sheet from the previous section on capitalization, is as follows:

$$\text{Book value} = \left(\begin{array}{c} \text{Common} \\ \text{stock} \end{array} + \begin{array}{c} \text{Capital} \\ \text{surplus} \end{array} + \begin{array}{c} \text{Retained} \\ \text{earnings} \end{array} - \text{Intangibles} \right) \div \begin{array}{c} \text{Number of} \\ \text{shares of} \\ \text{common stock} \\ \text{outstanding} \end{array}$$

Book value = ($300,000 + $100,000 + $260,000 − $10,000) ÷ $30,000 = $21.67 per share

The *book value per common share* represents the amount of cash that would be available for each share of common stock if all the assets (excepting intangibles) were sold *at the value at which they are carried on the balance sheet* and if all liabilities, bondholders, and preferred stockholders were also "paid off." For demonstration purposes, let us assume that the company must pay the bondholders and preferred stockholders the total par value of their securities as shown on the balance sheet. (Accountants would most probably use the higher value between the total par value as shown on the balance sheet and the total market value based on the call price of their securities.)

A company's book value can be of great significance, despite the fact that (in the real world) liquidating the company at balance sheet values is virtually impossible. An increasing book value is generally considered to be a healthy sign for a company whereas a decreasing book value may indicate a weakening financial situation. To the securities analyst, whether a company's book value is *increasing* or *decreasing* is especially significant. Normally, a company's *book value* and its *market value* bear no correlation (with some exceptions mostly for financial service companies, such as insurance firms), although these values *do* necessarily move in concert with each other. For example, the "bid" shown in the newspaper for mutual funds is *actually* the *book value* of a share of the fund.

Summary Comment

As we have seen, the balance sheet reflects the company's financial position at a particular point in time—what it owns, what it owes, and what the shareholders are worth. It is like a snapshot of a subject "on the run"—the action is frozen, and the values are reflected as of the close of business on the balance sheet date.

Although one balance sheet can be very revealing, a *series* of balance sheets, possibly covering the previous 5 or 6 years of operations, can be of even greater significance. The *trends* are extremely important. Is the present year's current ratio better or worse than it has been over the last several years? Is the book value per common share becoming higher or lower? A study of the ratios *over a period of a few years* can reveal much about the company's future prospects.

Let's review.

QUESTIONS

Answer the following questions using the balance sheet for XYZ Corporation.

XYZ MANUFACTURING CORPORATION

December 31, 1988

Assets		*Liabilities*	
Cash	$ 50,000	Accounts payable	$ 100,000
Marketable securities	84,000	Notes payable	85,000
Accounts receivable	268,000	Accrued expenses	95,000
Inventory	$ 254,000	Accrued taxes	$ 70,000
Total current assets	$ 656,000	Total current liabilities	$ 350,000
Property, plant, and equipment	462,000	Bonds 7%—due 1996	+250,000
		Total liabilities	$ 600,000
		Net Worth	
Prepayments	27,000	Preferred stock ($50 par)	50,000
		Common stock ($25 par)	100,000
		Paid-in capital	50,000
Intangibles	+ 30,000	Retained earnings	+375,000
		Total net worth	575,000
		Total liabilities and net worth	
Total assets	$1,175,000	worth	$1,175,000

1. What is the common stockholders' equity?
2. What is XYZ Corporation's capitalization?
3. What is the bond ratio?
4. What is the preferred stock ratio?
5. What is the common stock ratio?
6. What is the book value per share of common stock?

ANSWERS

1. | $525,000 |

Common stockholders' equity is determined by adding all three elements in the common stock account:

$$\text{Common stockholders' equity} = \text{Common Stock} + \text{Paid-in capital} + \text{Retained earnings}$$

$$= \$100,000 + \$50,000 + \$375,000$$

$$= \$525,000$$

Note: Do not confuse common stockholders' equity with shareholders' equity. The latter term (synonymous with net worth) includes the preferred stock as well.

2. | $825,000 |

Capitalization is derived by adding together the funded debt and the net worth.

$$\text{Capitalization} = \text{Bonds} + \text{Preferred stock} + \text{Common stock} + \text{Paid-in capital} + \text{Retained earnings}$$

$$= \$250,000 + \$50,000 + \$100,000 + \$50,000 + \$375,000$$

$$= \$825,000$$

3. | 30.3% |

Divide the funded debt by the total capitalization.

$$\text{Bond ratio} = \frac{\text{Bonds}}{\text{Total capitalization}}$$

$$= \frac{\$250,000}{\$825,000} = 0.303 \text{ or } 30.3\%$$

4. | 6.1% |

Divide the total par value of the preferred stock by the total capitalization.

$$\text{Preferred stock ratio} = \frac{\text{Preferred stock}}{\text{Total capitalization}}$$

$$= \frac{\$50,000}{\$825,000} = 0.061 \text{ or } 6.1\%$$

5. | 63.6% |

Divide the common stockholders' equity by the total capitalization.

$$\text{Common stock ratio} = \frac{\text{Common stock + Paid-in capital + Retained earnings}}{\text{Total capitalization}}$$

$$= \frac{\$100,000 + \$50,000 + \$375,000}{\$825,000} = 0.636 \text{ or } 63.6\%$$

As a check on your answers to the last three questions, add the three capitalization ratios together. They should add up to 100 percent.

Bond ratio	30.3%
Preferred stock ratio	6.1%
Common stock ratio	+ 63.6%
Capitalization	100.0%

6. $123.75

Book value is obtained by subtracting intangibles from the common stockholders' equity and then dividing by the number of common shares outstanding.

$$\text{Book value} = \left(\begin{array}{c} \text{Common} \\ \text{stock} \end{array} + \begin{array}{c} \text{Paid-in} \\ \text{capital} \end{array} + \begin{array}{c} \text{Retained} \\ \text{earnings} \end{array} - \text{Intangibles} \right) \div \begin{array}{c} \text{Number of} \\ \text{common} \\ \text{shares out-} \\ \text{standing} \end{array}$$

$$= (\$100,000 + \$50,000 + \$375,000 - \$30,000) \div 4,000$$

$$= \$123.75$$

The intangibles ($30,000) are listed as the *last* item under assets. We can determine the *number* of common shares outstanding by dividing the *total* par value of the common stock by the *par value per share*.

$$\begin{array}{c} \text{Number of shares} \\ \text{of common stock} \\ \text{outstanding} \end{array} = \frac{\text{Total par value}}{\text{Par value per share of common stock}}$$

$$= \frac{\$100,000}{\$25} = \$4,000$$

Income Statement Construction

Corporate annual reports traditionally show a balance sheet representing the corporation's financial picture on a particular day, usually the final day of the company's fiscal year. Most annual reports contain another financial statement in addition to the balance sheet—the income statement. The *income statement* (also known as the *profit and loss statement*) is a statement of income and expenses, usually over the *entire* year. It shows how much the company made or lost during the year. A typical, simplified income statement appears in Figure 4.8. (Assume 30,000 shares of common stock outstanding.) Review that statement briefly before we examine it entry by entry.

FIGURE 4.8   Income Statement for Roxbury Manufacturing Company

INCOME STATEMENT

ROXBURY MANUFACTURING COMPANY
January 1–December 31, 1988

Net sales	$2,000,000
Cost of goods sold	− 1,590,000
Selling, general, and administrative expenses	− 154,000
Depreciation	− 56,000
Operating income	$ 200,000
Other income	+ 7,500
Total income (earnings before interest and taxes [EBIT])	$ 207,500
Interest on bonds	− 40,000
Taxes (50% rate)	− 83,750
Net income	$ 83,750
Preferred dividends	− 4,500
Net earnings (earnings available for common stock)	$ 79,250

Net Sales

The *net sales* listing shows the amount of revenue that the company took in as a result of its manufacturing activities. "Net" reflects the fact that returned goods and discounts have been taken into account. If this were a nonmanufacturing enterprise (such as an airline or utility), net sales could be called *operating revenues*.

Cost of Goods Sold

Think of *cost of goods sold* as "factory" costs. It includes such factors as the cost of maintaining the manufacturing facilities, raw materials, and labor.

Selling, General, and Administrative Expenses

Selling, general, and administrative expenses include the cost of running the *sales* office of the company including corporate staff, office payroll, salespersons' commissions, advertising, and other such nonmanufacturing expenses.

Depreciation

The annual depreciation of the fixed assets appears in the category *depreciation*. This is a *noncash expense* because the assets may have been paid for well in the past, but are being "charged off" in small increments each year.

Operating Income

Subtracting the operating costs from net sales yields *operating income*. It is "factory" profit, because bond interest, taxes, or income from sources other than manufacturing have not yet been considered.

Other Income

Other income is income the company receives as dividends and/or interest on the marketable securities it may own. This item may also include other sources of income not related directly to the firm's operations, such as the sale of real estate (above book value) or rental income on unused land held for future use.

Total Income

Also known as *earnings before interest and taxes* (EBIT), the term *total income* is fairly self-explanatory.

Interest on Bonds

Almost as self-explanatory as total income is *interest on bonds;* this is the amount of money that the corporation pays out each year to service its outstanding bonds.

Taxes

Federal and state income taxes, for our purposes, can be estimated at roughly 50 percent. Therefore, 50 percent of ($207,500 − $40,000) is $83,750 in taxes.

Net Income

Also known as *net profit,* the listing *net income* represents all income and all expenses that have been weighed against each other. Only stockholders remain to be satisfied.

Preferred Dividends

Note that the corporation deducts its bond interest payments *before* figuring its tax liability. *Preferred dividend* payments, however, are *not* a deductible item and do not lower taxes.

Net Earnings

Net earnings, also known as *earnings available for common stock*, may be reinvested in the company and/or paid out to the common stockholders as cash dividends. Any amount *not* paid out as dividends increases the retained earnings account.

Income Statement Analysis

Like balance sheet ratios, important income statement ratios measure a company's financial strength and reflect the company's state of affairs. In the following analyses, refer to the income statement shown in Figure 4.8.

Expense Ratio (Operating Ratio)

The *expense ratio* (also known as the *operating ratio*) is an excellent measure of corporate efficiency and should therefore be compared with the results of previous years. An increasing expense ratio could indicate a company's loss of control over its costs.

$$\text{Expense ratio} = \frac{\text{Operating costs}}{\text{Net sales}}$$

$$\text{Expense ratio} = \frac{\text{Cost of goods sold} + \text{Selling, general, and administrative expenses} + \text{Depreciation}}{\text{Net sales}}$$

$$= \frac{\$1,590,000 + \$154,000 + \$56,000}{\$2,000,000} = 0.90 \text{ or } 90\%$$

Margin-of-Profit Ratio

Representing the complement of the expense ratio, the *margin-of-profit ratio* shows the percentage of the sales dollar *not* consumed by operating costs. It is derived by dividing operating income by net sales.

$$\text{Margin-of-profit ratio} = \frac{\text{Operating income}}{\text{Net sales}}$$

$$= \frac{\$200,000}{\$2,000,000} = 0.10 \text{ or } 10\%$$

Note that the margin-of-profit ratio plus the operating ratio equals 100 percent.

Cash Flow

Realizing that one of the operating expenses—depreciation—is "artificial," we could ask how much actual cash the company has available *before* it pays out any monies on preferred or common stock cash dividends. Depreciation is not actually "spent," at least not in the current year. Therefore cash flow is equal to the sum of net income and annual depreciation.

$$\text{Cash flow} = \text{Net income} + \text{Annual depreciation}$$

$$= \$83,750 + \$56,000 = \$139,750$$

Interest Coverage

When examining a company, we want to know how well it provides for the payment of interest coupons on its outstanding bonds. To discover this, divide total income (EBIT) by the interest on the bonds:

$$\text{Interest coverage} = \frac{\text{Total income (EBIT)}}{\text{Interest on bonds}}$$

$$= \frac{\$207,500}{\$40,000} = 5.2 \text{ times}$$

Interest coverage of over four times is usually considered a safe margin for the protection of a company.

Preferred Dividend Coverage

Another question is, How well are the preferred dividends covered by earnings? To find out, merely divide the net income by the preferred dividend requirements.

$$\text{Preferred dividend coverage} = \frac{\text{Net income}}{\text{Preferred dividends}}$$

$$= \frac{\$83,750}{\$4,500} = 18.6 \text{ times}$$

The calculation shows that the earnings cover the preferred dividends 18.6 times over the net income.

Primary Earnings per Share

The earnings-per-share ratio is probably the most widely used measure of how well a company's fortunes are faring. As a result, it is also the most widely advertised measure—the "bottom line." This important measurement is determined by dividing the net earnings (equal to net income minus preferred dividends) by the number of common shares outstanding.

$$\text{Primary earnings per share} = \frac{\text{Net earnings}}{\begin{array}{c}\text{Number of shares}\\ \text{of common stock outstanding}\end{array}}$$

$$= \frac{\$79,250}{30,000} = \$2.64$$

The expression "earnings per share" has practically been replaced by the more modern expression *primary earnings per share*.

The newer term reflects earnings as they would be if all "common stock equivalents" were issued and outstanding as is common stock, thereby diluting "ordinary" earning per share by 3 percent or more. Common stock equivalents include *certain* warrants, stock options, convertible bonds, and convertible preferred shares. Common stock equivalents, if they exist, are clearly labeled. Corporations now report primary earnings per share so that the investing public does *not* have to refigure the "ordinary" earnings per share. The public does not have to determine which convertible items are considered common stock equivalents. When earnings are figured to include *all* possible additional shares of common stock (whether common stock equivalents or not), then such earnings are reported as "fully diluted."

Fully Diluted Earnings per Share

A corporation may have convertible bonds and/or convertible preferred stock outstanding. Investors realize that earnings per common share would be affected if such securities were to be converted. Fully diluted earnings reflect the per-share results as they *would* be if all *potential* common shares were added to the outstanding common stock. Under this method all warrants, stock options (options issued *privately* by the corporation), and convertible issues are considered as if they were exchanged for additional common stock.

Figure 4.9 contains the same basic figures as those shown in Figure 4.8, but they have been recalculated based on the assumption that the outstanding bonds are convertible, and that they *have been* converted. The bonds are convertible into 20,000 additional shares of stock. Additionally, the corporate tax rate is 50 percent. Assuming that the convertible bonds are exchanged for common stock, the interest on bonds entry disappears. With this disappearance of a $40,000 deduction, the income *before* tax rises from $167,500 to $207,500. At a tax rate of 50 percent, the tax burden under fully diluted conditions is $103,750, instead of $83,750. This increases net earnings from $79,250 to $99,250. Assuming again that the bonds are converted, we must take into account the additional shares thus created. If 30,000 shares were outstanding before the conversion, then the fully diluted earnings figure is calculated by dividing the "new" net earnings by 50,000 shares of common stock (30,000 outstanding + 20,000 after conversion). Of course, all these changes affect the "ordinary" earnings per share of the corporation.

$$\frac{\text{Fully diluted}}{\text{earnings per share}} = \frac{\text{Net earnings}}{\text{Number of shares of common stock outstanding after conversion}}$$

$$= \frac{\$99,250}{50,000} = \$1.99$$

FIGURE 4.9   Income Statement (Fully Diluted)

INCOME STATEMENT
(Fully Diluted)

ROXBURY MANUFACTURING COMPANY
January 1–December 31, 1988

Net sales	$2,000,000
Cost of goods sold	− 1,590,000
Selling, general, and administrative expenses	− 154,000
Depreciation	− 56,000
Operating income	$ 200,000
Other income	+ 7,500
Total income (earnings before interest and taxes [EBIT])	$ 207,500
Taxes (50% rate)	− 103,750
Net income	$ 103,750
Preferred dividends	− 4,500
Net earnings (earnings available for common stock)	$ 99,250

Test your knowledge of income statements.

QUESTIONS

1. Prepare an income statement from the following information. We have purposely included information that is irrelevant. Some of the items listed don't even belong on a corporate income statement. So pick and choose carefully. Answer *all* questions using the following information. (Figure taxes at 50 percent.)

Interest on debt paid	$ 402,600
Preferred dividends paid	26,050
Other income	68,500
Common stock dividends paid	540,000
Depreciation	630,000
Current liabilities	3,200,000
Net sales	16,500,000
Taxes paid	1,167,450
Selling, general and administrative expenses	1,413,000
Cost of goods sold	11,788,000
Number of shares of common stock outstanding	600,000

2. What is the expense (operating) ratio?

3. What is the margin-of-profit ratio?

4. What is the cash flow?

5. What are the earnings per share (assuming there are *no* common stock equivalents)?

6. Assume that the outstanding bonds are convertible into 200,000 additional shares of stock. What would be the fully diluted earnings per share? (Assume a 50 percent tax rate.)

ANSWERS

1.

Net sales	$16,500,000
Cost of goods sold	− 11,788,000
Selling, general, and administrative expenses	− 1,413,000
Depreciation	− 630,000
Operating income	2,669,000
Other income	+ 68,500
Total income (EBIT)	2,737,500
Interest on bonds	− 402,600
Taxes	− 1,167,450
Net income	1,167,450
Preferred dividends	− 26,050
Net earnings (earnings available for common stock)	$ 1,141,400

The amount of common stock dividends paid does *not* appear on the income statement, nor do current liabilities and the number of shares of common stock outstanding. However, the common stock outstanding *is* required when figuring earnings per share.

2. $\boxed{83.8\%}$

$$\text{Expense (operating) ratio} = \frac{\text{Operating costs}}{\text{Net sales}}$$

$$= \frac{\text{Cost of goods sold} + \dfrac{\text{Selling, general, and administrative expenses}}{\text{Net sales}} + \text{Depreciation}}{}$$

$$= \frac{\$11,788,000 + \$1,413,000 + \$630,000}{\$16,500,000}$$

$$= 0.838 \text{ or } 83.8\%$$

3. | 16.2% |

$$\text{Margin-of-profit ratio} = \frac{\text{Operating income}}{\text{Net sales}}$$

$$= \frac{\$2,669,000}{\$16,500,000}$$

$$= 0.162 \text{ or } 16.2\%$$

As a check on yourself, add the expense ratio and margin of profit together. They are complements and *should* add up to 100 percent:

Expense ratio	83.8%
Margin of profit	+16.2%
	100.0%

It appears that our calculations are correct.

4. | $1,797,450 |

$$\text{Cash flow} = \text{Net income} + \text{Depreciation}$$
$$= \$1,167,450 + \$630,000$$
$$= \$1,797,450$$

Remember to add the annual depreciation to *net income,* not to net earnings.

5. | $1.90 |

$$\text{Earnings per share} = \frac{\text{Net earnings}}{\text{Number of shares of common stock outstanding}}$$

$$= \frac{\$1,141,400}{600,000}$$

$$= \$1.90$$

Note: Net earnings is determined by subtracting preferred dividends from net income.

6. | $1.68 |

The income statement has to be recalculated, giving effect to the conversion of the bonds. This will (1) eliminate the "interest on bonds" figure, (2) raise taxes, and (3) create a greater number of common shares outstanding. The income statement prepared as an answer to question 1 remains the same (up to and including the figure for total income). Let us prepare the "fully diluted" income statement from this point:

Total income (EBIT)	$2,737,500
Taxes	− 1,368,750
Net income	1,368,750
Preferred dividends	− 26,050
Net earnings (earnings available for common stock)	$1,342,700

Note the changes from the "original" income statement given for question 1. In this particular question the bonds are convertible. We must *eliminate* the "interest on bonds" charge. This makes the entire total income figure subject to taxation. Net income is now $1,368,750.

To figure earnings per share, subtract preferred dividends (if any) from net income, and divide by the number of common shares outstanding. Thus:

$$\text{Fully diluted earnings per share} = \frac{\text{Net earnings}}{\text{Number of shares of common stock outstanding}}$$

$$= \frac{\$1,342,700}{800,000} = \$1.68$$

We are *now* using 800,000 as the number of common shares outstanding; we arrived at this figure by adding the 200,000 shares that *would* be issued in exchange for the bonds to the already outstanding 600,000 shares.

Other Analyses

Payout Ratio

Most corporations pay out at least a part of their net earnings to common shareholders through cash dividends. The percentage of earnings thereby distributed is known as the *payout ratio*. As a rough guideline, growth companies may be expected to have low payout ratios (10 percent), as compared to a typical manufacturing company payout of approximately 50 percent. This ratio is derived by dividing the total common dividends paid by the total net earnings (net income minus preferred dividends).

EXAMPLE

$$\text{Payout ratio} = \frac{\text{Common stock dividends}}{\text{Net income} - \text{Preferred dividends}}$$

A corporation with $1,000,000 in net income pays $50,000 in preferred dividends and $375,000 in common stock dividends. Its payout ratio is:

$$\text{Payout ratio} = \frac{\$375,000}{\$1,000,000 - \$50,000} = 0.394 \text{ or } 39.4\%$$

Yield on Common Stock

To determine *current yield,* divide a security's annual dividends (or coupons) by its current market price.

$$\text{Current yield} = \frac{\text{Annual dividend rate}}{\text{Market price}}$$

Generally speaking, companies with greater prospects for growth have lower yields, since growth companies usually reinvest most of their earnings in their own business.

EXAMPLE

A common stock has a current market price of $42 and pays annual dividends of $1.80. Its current yield is 4.3 percent, calculated as follows:

$$\text{Current yield} = \frac{\$1.80}{\$42} = 0.043 \text{ or } 4.3\%$$

Inventory Turnover Ratio

We can measure how effectively a company is selling its products by determining how often its supply of inventory is manufactured and sold. Of the several methods for calculating this ratio, the simplest (and probably least professional) is as follows:

$$\boxed{\text{Inventory turnover ratio} = \frac{\text{Net sales}}{\text{Year-end inventory}}}$$

This method is presented because it is simple and workable. Other methods use the cost of goods sold rather than net sales as the numerator of the fraction and the *average* inventory, rather than year-end inventory, as the denominator. As a general guide, a "good" inventory turnover ratio for an average manufacturing company is 6 times per year (on average).

EXAMPLE

A corporation's annual report shows net sales of $14,000,000 (on the income statement) and an inventory of $2,682,000 (on the balance sheet). The inventory turnover is 5.2 times, determined as follows:

$$\text{Inventory turnover ratio} = \frac{\$14,000,000}{\$2,682,000} = 5.2 \text{ times}$$

Price/Earnings Ratio

The *price/earnings,* or *P/E,* ratio is one of the most significant measurements. It relates a corporation's profitability to the market price of its common shares and affords us a measure of the *relative* "expensiveness" of the common stock. Typically, growth stocks have high P/E ratios. Companies with slower growth prospects sell at lower earnings multiples. To obtain this ratio, divide the market price of the company's common stock by the earnings per share as in the following:

$$\boxed{\text{Price/earnings ratio} = \frac{\text{Current market price of the common stock}}{\text{Common stock earnings per share}}}$$

EXAMPLE

Company A earned $1.04 per share. Its common stock is selling in the open market at 23¼.

$$\text{Price/earnings (P/E) ratio} = \frac{\$23.25}{\$1.04} = 22.4$$

Each share of common stock is selling for about 22 times the amount of earnings generated by each share.

Let's review again.

QUESTIONS

Answer all questions from the information presented.

XYZ CORPORATION:

Market prices (current):		
Common stock	84	
Preferred stock	96	
Net income		$1,875,000
Number of shares of common stock outstanding		250,000
Number of share of preferred stock outstanding		50,000
Annual dividends per share:		
Common stock	$3.75	
Preferred stock	6.00	

1. What are XYZ Corporation's earnings per share?
2. What is the price/earnings (P/E) ratio?
3. What is the payout ratio?
4. What is the current yield on the preferred stock?
5. What is the current yield on the common stock?

ANSWERS

1. $6.30

$$\text{Earnings per share} = \frac{\text{Net income} - \text{Preferred dividends}}{\text{Number of common shares outstanding}}$$

$$= \frac{\$1,875,000 - \$300,000}{\$250,000}$$

$$= \$6.30$$

We can determine that the preferred dividend requirements were $300,000 since there are 50,000 preferred shares outstanding, with each share paying a $6 dividend.

2. 13.3

$$\text{Price/earnings ratio} = \frac{\text{Market price of common stock}}{\text{Common stock earnings per share}}$$

$$= \frac{\$84}{\$6.30}$$

$$= 13.3$$

3. 59.5%

$$\text{Payout ratio} = \frac{\text{Common stock dividends}}{\text{Earnings available for common stock}}$$

$$= \frac{\$937,500}{\$1,575,000}$$

$$= 0.595 \text{ or } 59.5\%$$

$$\text{Common stock dividends} = \begin{array}{l} \text{Total common shares} \\ \times \text{ Dividends per share} \end{array}$$

$$= 250{,}000 \times \$3.75$$

$$= \$937{,}500$$

$$\begin{array}{l} \text{Earnings available for} \\ \text{common stock} \end{array} = \text{Net income} - \text{Preferred dividends}$$

$$= \$1{,}875{,}000 - \$300{,}000$$

$$= \$1{,}575{,}000$$

We figure payout ratio on a *per-share* basis, rather than on a gross basis.

$$\text{Payout ratio} = \frac{\text{Dividends per common share}}{\text{Earnings per common share}}$$

$$= \frac{\$3.75}{\$6.30}$$

$$= 0.595 \text{ or } 59.5\%$$

4. | 6.3% |

$$\text{Current yield} = \frac{\text{Annual dividend}}{\text{Market price}}$$

$$= \frac{\$6}{\$96}$$

$$= 0.063 \text{ or } 6.3\%$$

5. | 4.5% |

$$\text{Current yield} = \frac{\text{Annual dividend}}{\text{Market price}}$$

$$= \frac{\$3.75}{\$84}$$

$$= 0.045 \text{ or } 4.5\%$$

Note that the method of figuring *current* yield is the same for both common and preferred stock. In both instances, the annual dividend is divided by the current market price for that particular security.

Return on Equity

An informative measure of management's efficiency is the *return on equity*, derived by dividing net income by shareholders' equity. (Shareholders' equity is the sum of preferred stock, common stock, paid-in capital, and retained earnings.)

$$\text{Return on equity} = \frac{\text{Net income}}{\text{Shareholders' equity}}$$

EXAMPLE

Turn to the balance sheet in Figure 4.1 and to the income statement in Figure 4.8. Using the information from those statements, the return is calculated as follows:

$$\text{Return on equity} = \frac{\$83,750}{\$735,000} = 0.114 \text{ or } 11.4\%$$

Return on Invested Capital

A measure of how well the company is utilizing its entire capitalization is the *return on invested capital*. (For a review of how the total capitalization figure is derived, see the section "Capitalization (Capital Structure–Invested Capital)."

The formula is:

$$\text{Return on invested capital} = \frac{\text{Net income} + \text{Interest on debt}}{\text{Total capitalization (invested capital)}}$$

EXAMPLE

Using the balance sheet and the income statement in Figures 4.1 and 4.8, calculate the interest on bonds ($40,000) by multiplying the coupon rate (8 percent) by the total par value, $500,000. After that, fill in the formula:

$$\text{Return on invested capital} = \frac{\$83,750 + \$40,000}{\$1,235,000}$$

$$= 10.0\%$$

"Financial Reasoning" Problems

Let us apply our knowledge by following the effects of a managerial decision on the corporation's financial statements. In each instance, we shall trace the course of events, noting the impact on the company's assets, liabilities, shareholders' equity, and several of the more common ratios.

Stock Splits

When a common stock is split, the *number of shares* of common stock *increases,* and the *par value* of the common stock *decreases* in the same proportion.

EXAMPLE

A "beginning" common stockholders' equity before a split consists of:

Common stock: at $.40 par value, 600,000 shares authorized, 300,000 shares issued and outstanding	$120,000
Paid-in capital	40,000
Retained earnings	+ 135,000
Total common stockholders' equity	$295,000

In a 2-for-1 split, the number of issued and outstanding shares doubles (from 300,000 to 600,000), and the par value is halved (from $.40 to $.20). The *new* common stockholders' equity looks like this after the split:

Common stock: at $.20 par value, 600,000 shares author- ized, 600,000 shares issued and outstanding	$120,000
Paid-in capital	40,000
Retained earnings	+ 135,000
Total common stockholders' equity	$295,000

Because of the 2-for-1 split, the par value changes from $.40 to $.20, but the number of outstanding shares doubles. No *real* change occurs in the balance sheet. The common stock account is *still* $120,000:

300,000 shares @ $.40 per = $120,000
and
600,000 shares @ $.20 per = $120,000

Certainly a greater number of shares are outstanding; but (at least in theory) the shareholders are no better off (and no *worse* off) than they were before the split. Market theory suggests that the stock will sell better at a *lower price* after the split because it is more "marketable." People tend to favor lower-priced issues even though a lower-priced security bears no more intrinsic value than a higher-priced security. The actual net effect of the split is nil, since the book values on the balance sheet do not change.

Stock Dividends

Classically, stock dividends require the issuance of additional shares, but the par value of the common stock does *not* change.

EXAMPLE

Using the stockholders' equity statement from the previous section, let us restate the figures as they appear after the payment of a 30 percent stock dividend, that is, 90,000 shares (30% of 300,000):

Common stock: at $.40 par value, 600,000 shares author- $156,000
    ized, 390,000 shares issued and outstanding

Paid-in capital   40,000

Retained earnings   +   99,000

    Total common stockholders' equity $295,000

Compare the previous figures with these. The *total* equity does not change. Nevertheless, the common stock account increases by $36,000 (from $120,000 to $156,000), and the retained earnings account decreases by $36,000 (from $135,000 to $99,000). Our common stockholders are not richer or poorer, but the balance sheet changes in that the common stock account increases at the expense of the retained earnings account.

Smaller stock dividends (generally less than 25 percent) are treated differently. Paid-in capital may also be increased, and the market value of the common stock may be taken into account.

Declaration of Cash Dividends

A board of directors announces a cash dividend payment of $0.50 per common share approximately two months before the dividends are actually paid out to the stockholders. As a result, the ABC Corporation balance sheet in Figure 4.10 undergoes changes between the time the corporation declares a cash dividend and the time it actually pays it (use the balance sheet in Figure 4.10 for the remainder of this section).

The declaration of a cash dividend creates a current liability of $6,000 ($0.50 × 12,000 common shares). Current liabilities must be adjusted to include this *new* obligation, which must be paid out within the next year. An item (probably labeled "dividends payable") is added to current liabilities, raising the total by $6,000 to $477,000. Where does this $6,000 come from? It comes from the accumulated retained earnings. As you will recall, retained earnings may be thought of as unpaid dividends. Management has now decided to pay some of this accumulated value to the common stockholders. We now *reduce* retained earnings by $6,000 (from $290,000 to $284,000). The overall "change" on the balance sheet is an increase in current liabilities and a decrease in retained earnings.

Since current assets remain the same while current liabilities have

FIGURE 4.10   Balance Sheet for ABC Corporation

BALANCE SHEET

ABC CORPORATION
June 30, 1988

Assets		*Liabilities*	
Cash	$165,000	Accounts payable	$166,000
Marketable securities	18,000	Accrued taxes	70,000
Accounts receivable	260,000	Notes payable	84,000
Inventory	455,000	Accrued expenses	151,000
Total current assets	$898,000	Total current liabilities	$471,000
		First mortgage bonds:	500,000
		7½%—due 1/1/94	
		Total liabilities	$971,000

Property, plant, and equipment:

		Stockholders' Equity	
Land	$ 75,000		
Buildings	506,000		
Equipment	89,000	Preferred stock	100,000
Machinery	164,000	($100 par)	
	834,000	1,000 shares author-ized, issued, and outstanding	
Less: Accumulated depre-ciation	– 217,000	Common stock ($25 par) 12,000 shares author-ized, issued, and	300,000
Net property, plant, and equipment	$ 617,000	outstanding	
Intangibles	204,000	Paid-in capital	58,000
		Accumulated retained earnings	290,00
Total assets	$1,719,000	Total stockholders' equity	$748,000
		Total liabilities and stockholders' equity	$1,719,000

increased, several ratios are adversely affected. The dividend reduces the following:

Working capital (net current assets)

Quick asset ratio (acid test ratio)

Current ratio

Book value

Logically, the dividend also reduces the common stockholders' stake in the company because part of their accumulated profits is paid out to them. Understandably, the value remaining after they receive their dividends is reduced by the amount of such dividends.

Payment of Cash Dividends

When the ABC Corporation actually pays out the cash dividends, the company is dispersing cash in the amount of the current liability established for such payment. The following changes occur:

Cash decreases.

Dividends payable disappears.

Cash is now $159,000 ($165,000 − $6,000), and total current assets decreases to $892,000. The total current liabilities entry goes back to $471,000. Note where the *ultimate* change occurs. Cash is reduced, and the payment comes from retained earnings. The shift was done in two stages:

Stage 1. When the dividend is *declared,* retained earnings decrease and current liabilities increase.

Stage 2. When the dividend is *paid,* cash decreases and that particular current liability disappears.

Retiring Debt at a Discount

If the corporation's bonds are trading in the open market at a discount, the management may possibly elect to buy them back. Thus they can retire the obligation at a bargin rate rather than pay the holders full *par value* at maturity.

The ABC Corporation buys $50,000 of its own bonds in the open market for a total of $40,000. The balance sheet changes as follows:

Cash decreases by *$40,000*.

Total current assets and *total* assets also decrease by the same amount.

Working capital, quick assets, current ratio, and the acid-test (quick asset) ratio all decline because current assets are reduced while current liabilities remain unchanged.

Bonds are reduced by $50,000.

Stockholders' equity *increases* by $10,000 because we have reduced assets (cash) by $40,000 and liabilities by $50,000; we gain $10,000, which is reflected in increased net worth. Since the company has "paid off" a $50,000 debt at a cost of only $40,000, the stockholders have gained.

Although the *cash* picture is not as good as it was and some ratios have declined, the overall effect is "good" in that stockholders' equity increases.

Retiring Debt at a Premium

The ABC Corporation elects to retire some of its bonds through the exercise of a "call" provision. The call price is usually above par, so the corporation is paying a premium price for the early retirement of part of its debt. Calling $100,000 par value of bonds at a price of 102 ($1,020 per bond) costs the corporation $102,000. Management is eliminating a $100,000 debt (liabilities), but the cost is $102,000 in cash (assets). It pays the "extra" $2,000 from retained earnings.

Note the effects on the corporation's balance sheet. Cash decreases from $165,000 to $63,000. Current assets now total only $796,000 and total assets are $1,617,000. On the liabilities side of the balance sheet, the bonds go down from $500,000 to $400,000 and total liabilities from $971,000 to $871,000. Retained earnings reflect the $2,000 "loss" the company suffered and decrease from $290,000 to $288,000. The "new" balance sheet shows:

Total assets = Total liabilities + Net worth (stockholders' equity)
$1,617,000 = $871,000 + $746,000

The cash spent also adversely affects working capital, current ratio, quick assets, and the liquidity (quick asset) ratio.

Sale and Lease-Back of Fixed Assets

The ABC Corporation decides to raise cash by selling and leasing back some of its expensive machinery. The corporation sells machinery carried on its balance sheet at $30,000. This sale reduces the property, plant, and equipment from $617,000 to $587,000. At the same time it increases current assets from $898,000 to $928,000 because cash goes up to $195,000.

The effect on the balance sheet depends on whether the sale is made at a price greater or lower than the value at which the assets are carried on the balance sheet. Essentially, if the sale is made for more than the book value of the asset, the corporation makes a "profit." For sales of assets at prices below their book value, the corporation sustains a "loss." In essence, the company is exchanging a *fixed* asset (machinery) for a *current* asset (cash). This shift increases current assets at the expense of fixed assets and thus improves working capital and the current ratio. Since current assets increase while current liabilities remain the same, the corporation's working capital increases (current assets minus current liabilities). Also, the current ratio (current assets divided by current liabilities) also improves. In short:

If the asset is sold at a profit, total assets increase, and the increase is also reflected in the retained earnings account.

If the asset is sold at a loss, total assets decrease (by the difference between the book value and the sale price of the asset sold). The decrease also lowers the retained earnings account by the same amount.

Glossary of Important Formulas and Terms

To help you review the many formulas in this chapter, an alphabetical listing follows. The page numbers in parentheses will enable you to refer to the text when necessary.

Acid Test Ratio   *See* Quick Asset Ratio. (84)

Annual Depreciation   That portion of the cost of fixed assets charged as an expense for a given year. (87)

Balance Sheet Equation   Total assets equal total liabilities plus stockholders' equity. (73)

Bond Ratio   Bonds divided by total capitalization. (107) *See also* Capitalization. (105)

Book Value per Share   Common stockholders' equity minus intangible assets divided by number of common shares outstanding. (108) *See also* Common Stockholders' Equity.

Capitalization   Bonds plus preferred stock plus common stock plus paid-in capital plus retained earnings. (105)

Capital Surplus   *See* Paid-in Capital. (101)

Cash Flow   Net income plus annual depreciation. (118)

Common Stock Ratio   Common stock plus capital surplus plus retained earnings divided by total capitalization. (107)

Common Stockholders' Equity   Common stock plus paid-in capital plus retained earnings. (108)

Current Ratio   Current assets divided by current liabilities. (83)

Current Yield   *See* Yield on Common Stock. (127)

Depreciation   *See* Straight-Line Depreciation, Sum-of-Years' Digits Depreciation, and Double-Declining-Balance Depreciation. *See also* Annual Depreciation. (87)

Earned Surplus   *See* Retained Earnings. (102)

Earning per Share   *See* Primary Earnings per Share. (119)

Expense Ratio   Operating costs divided by net sales. (117)

Funded Debt   Outstanding bonds maturing five years or more in the future. (98)

Income Statement   Shows how much a company made or lost during the year. (114)

Interest Coverage   Total income divided by interest on bonds. (118)

Inventory Turnover   Net sales divided by year-end inventory. (127)

Liquidity Ratio   *See* Quick Asset Ratio. (84)

Margin-of-Profit Ratio   Operating income divided by net sales. (117)

Net Cost   Actual cost minus salvage value. (88)
Net Current Assets   *See* Working Capital. (82)
Net Earnings   Net income minus preferred dividends. (117)
Net Working Capital   *See* Working Capital. (82)
Operating Ratio   *See* Expense Ratio. (117)
Paid-in Capital   The amount of money the company received from the sale of shares of common stock to the public in addition to the par value. (101)
Payout Ratio   Common stock dividends divided by net income minus preferred dividends. (126)
Preferred Dividend Coverage   Net income divided by preferred dividends. (119)
Preferred Stock Ratio   Preferred stock divided by total capitalization. (107)
Price/Earnings Ratio (P/E)   Current market price of the common stock divided by the common stock earnings per share. (128)
Primary Earnings per Share   Net earnings divided by number of shares of common stock outstanding. (119)
Profit and Loss Statement   *See* Income Statement. (114)
Profit Margin Ratio   *See* Margin of Profit Ratio. (117)
Quick Assets   Total current assets minus inventory. (79)
Quick Asset Ratio   Quick assets divided by current liabilities. (84)
Retained Earnings   Amount of profit the company has retained in the business after any dividends have been paid. (102)
Return on Equity   Net income divided by shareholders' equity. (132)
Return on Invested Capital   Net income plus interest on debt divided by total capitalization. (132)
Total Capitalization   *See* Capitalization. (105)
Working Capital   Current assets minus current liabilities. (82)
Yield on Common Stock   Annual dividend rate divided by market price. (127)

Concluding Comments

We have explained the construction of the two most *basic* financial statements, the balance sheet and the income statement. We trust that you now understand the basic purpose of each document and can examine such statements with an eye toward evaluating a company's future prospects.

These documents detail a corporation's financial position and its earnings. They show the end result of the management's efforts to run a profitable business. Knowing how to interpret this information is essential to a professional analysis of the company—the key ingredient to enable you to decide whether to buy or sell the company's securities.

5

Types
of Stock
and Their
Valuation

PART I

Investment Objectives

In most of this work we have focused our attention on investments
for the *individual* and contrasted these investment "policies" with
those of the *institutional* buyer. This chapter will continue this individual focus. We will briefly consider each of the types of stock
available and present the basics of common stock valuation.

In terms of the average size of holdings, it has become obvious
that financial institutions are the largest group in the investment
industry. As we have shown, their policies are well standardized, and
the architectural framework of their decisions is tempered by their
obligations and "representative" behavior. Patterns followed by
individuals tend to be much less consistent and certainly not as
clear-cut.

The needs of individual investors vary greatly with their circumstances. History has shown that there is a certain "parallelism"
between these buyers and the classes of institutions that have evolved
around them. Face it, investments made on behalf of widows and

orphans are *far* more conservative than those made for multi-millionaires. But, these trends have changed in recent years as the threat of inflation and the overall need for higher income have changed even these *widow-and-orphan* portfolios.

In the previous chapter we outlined how common stocks fit in with the overall financial picture of a business. Stocks represent the shares of ownership in a business. Each share represents the ownership of a certain percentage of the firm, depending on the number of shares that are outstanding. For example, if there are 100 shares outstanding for the firm, each share of stock represents a 1 percent ownership of the firm. Typically, firms have millions of shares outstanding. Individuals who own 5 percent or more of the company stock are called *major shareholders*.

The rise or fall of stock price (value) is governed by the success or failure of the company. When a company's profits increase, so does the total value of its stock. The increase in stock value makes investment in the company profitable. It is important, however, to understand how the "business" operates, since there are several types of business organizations—proprietorships, partnerships, and corporations. Only corporations may issue stocks to investors.

Common Stock

Most frequently, the term *stock* refers to *common stock*. There are various kinds of stock, however, and it is imperative that investors be familiar with each type. Companies that *go public* issue common stock to the investing public. Essentially, they offer the public a chance to own part of the corporation through purchase of this stock. Most stocks traded on the exchanges are common stock. When you purchase this stock, you become part owner of the corporation through an *equity investment*. As the company prospers, the stock value increases, and, conversely, as a company's profits decline, it is very probable that the price of the stock will follow suit. Each time you purchase a share of stock in a company, you essentially cast a vote of confidence in its future growth and profitability.

The return on investment (ROI) comes to you in stock price appreciation, which is also called *capital gains*. Stockholders also receive an ROI in the form of dividends on the stock they hold. Even though companies are not obligated to pay dividends, many corporations choose to do so—particularly those with mature businesses or those in regulated industries (e.g., utilities). Shareholders in these companies focus on cash dividends, whereas individuals who hold stock in rapidly growing businesses tend to prefer that they retain their earnings for expansion. In some cases, dividends are paid in the form of *additional* stock, although when this occurs, each shareholder's percentage of *total* ownership does *not* increase.

As a shareholder, you have certain rights and privileges that accompany stock ownership. Federal law requires a public company to supply its shareholders with timely reports of the company's financial condition. These reports are usually published on a quarterly or yearly basis. Shareholders must be notified of any significant event(s) that could affect the company [e.g., resignation of a senior officer or corporate property loss by fire, theft, or act of God (tornado, hurricane, and so forth)].

Company management must acquire the votes of its shareholders on a yearly basis in the form of *proxy statements* to support the continuation of in-place management. Additionally, the stockholdings of all company officials and directors, major stockholders (5 percent holdings or greater), and compensation paid to management must be made *public*. Corporate charter changes must be approved by stockholders. Public corporations must also hold annual meetings of shareholders to provide owners with a forum for expressing individual views and opinions about the company.

Common stock enjoys easy transfer of ownership—*transferability*. It is this easy exchange of ownership that creates an active and dynamic market. For that matter, common stocks are one of the most *liquid* forms of individual investment. It should be noted, however, that in cases where a company goes bankrupt, common stockholders are *subordinated* to the claims of all creditors (Uncle Sam is number one on this list if back taxes are owed) and the preferred shareholders. As a holder of a "piece of the action," you stand to gain or to lose in accordance with the company's good or bad fortune.

What is *par value?* Most corporations assign a *par value* to their common stock. Today, this has little significance, although in the past it was commonplace for companies to assign a value to each share when the company went public. Today, this value is used only

for bookkeeping; for all practical purposes, this value is *not* correlated with a stock's book value or its market value.

When a business is incorporated, its management decides the
manner in which it will *authorize* the company to issue shares. In
many instances, companies authorize a larger number of shares than
they plan to offer *initially*. When this tactic is used, additional shares
can be offered in the future. Until they are offered, these shares are
known as *authorized-but-unissued* shares. Management can authorize increases in the number of shares with stockholder approval.
Issued-and-outstanding shares are those distributed among investors.

What is a stock *warrant?* In order to make new stock more
attractive, a corporation may attach a warrant to the common shares
being issued. This type of issue allows the shareholder to hold a
long-term privilege to *subscribe* to common stock at a *fixed* price.
The price at which shares can be purchased is called the exercise
price. In most cases the exercise price is set higher than the offering
price. The investor holding warrants makes gains whenever the price
of the security increases after it is issued.

Shares can also be reacquired by a company; this occurs when
company management purchases back a stock or if management is
attempting to prevent an unfriendly takeover. Reacquired shares are
called *treasury stock*. For the common stock shareholder, a repurchase can prevent the stock price from "bottoming out" since a
major repurchase provides a "floor" for the price, causing it to
stabilize. The company itself most likely represents the wealthiest
obtainable buyer. However, a repurchase program creates *less* stock
liquidity, can inhibit a takeover, and in some cases can *perpetuate*
incompetent management!

Another term used frequently by stock experts is *float*. The *float*
represents the number of shares outstanding minus the number of
shares held by corporate insiders—the number of shares *available*
then for trading on the open market. It is important to understand
the float and use it as a measure of insider control. Similarly, the float
helps investors determine how difficult or easy it would be to
accumulate a position (purchase or sell a large percentage of company stock).

Since common stocks are a popular investment, they are a very
diverse and liquid form of investment, and the potential gains are
great. However, the risk of common stocks is also greater than other
investments.

Preferred Stock

Preferred stocks, which combine the benefits of common stock and bonds, first became popular in the 1920s and 1930s as a hybrid equity investment. Preferred stock represents an equity investment in the ownership of a corporation, but to a limited degree. As a preferred stockholder, you have no voice in the selection of a company's officers and directors. However, you are promised a fixed dividend that takes precedence over any dividends paid to common stockholders. Preferred stockholders have a more senior claim on company assets in the event of liquidation or bankruptcy. Naturally, bondholders and creditors are first in line before preferred stockholders in these cases. Preferred stocks also have some *negative* aspects. Common stockholders enjoy the benefits of rising dividends and increased fortune as the company prospers. Preferred stockholders do not enjoy these benefits, and for this reason, they are very concerned with the dividends paid on these stocks. Increases in prevailing interest rates have a greater impact on preferred stock than they do on common stock.

Cumulative preferred stock and *convertible preferred stock* offer some attractive alternatives to the acquisition of capital gains. With *cumulative preferred stock,* the dividend accumulates and becomes a debt of the company in the years in which the company is unable to pay a preferred dividend. No dividend on common stock can be paid as long as the company owes the preferred dividend. For the knowledgeable and astute investor, the purchase of cumulative preferred stock with a *substantial* dividend owed can mean a possible "windfall profit" when the company's condition improves, and it pays all outstanding preferred dividends *before* paying dividends on its common stocks.

Convertible preferred stock promises investors a fixed dividend payment with the option of converting from preferred to common stock if and when the company becomes recognized in the market with a resultant appreciation of its common stock. In general, convertible preferreds (as they are commonly called) are more volatile that "straight" preferreds, since the market price is dependent on overall market performance of the common stock to which they can be converted.

Preferred stock purchasers are usually risk averters and are concerned about current income. Since federal tax laws allow many corporations and some institutional investors to shelter parts of the dividends they secure from their stock holdings, there is an additional incentive for certain investors to buy this type of stock.

What Are Blue Chip Stocks?

Common stocks of well-known companies are known as *blue chip stocks,* since these companies have histories of profit growth and dividend payment. Such companies are usually well managed and offer a variety of high-quality products and services. Blue chips are marked by high price and low yield. Astute investors who follow blue chip performance should look for sharp downturns in market performance to purchase blue chips at "bargain basement" prices. These stocks rally quickly and regain losses in many cases. We have already mentioned how IBM and Union Carbide stock rallied after disasters caused by market losses (Black Monday for IBM) and disaster (Bhopal for Union Carbide).

What Are the Characteristics of a Growth Stock?

Simply put, a company *or* its stock that shows rapid earnings increases over a few years is a growth company or a growth stock. Recently, the first companies to license a reliable test for AIDS in the general population became rapid growth *prospects* in the drug and medical treatment industry. In order to analyze growth you must be able to dissect a company's balance sheet. Growth situations exhibit certain characteristics, and in many cases the investor needs a crystal ball to gaze into future performance.

Discernment of the *trends in earnings and sales* is the key to recognizing growth companies. You must be able to get a "reading" on management's ability to achieve its defined goals. In many cases growth companies have weak or relatively poor balance sheets due to the fact that they are not concentrating on an asset base to meet the financial demands of developing products and services. By calculating the *growth on equity* and *total assets,* the *growth rate in dividends and earnings,* and the *price/earnings ratio,* the investor can obtain a quick analysis of the expected growth of a company's sales, earnings, and expenses. These are the milestones of growth, and we emphasize that there must be a trend—a predominant pattern—before one can label a company in a growth situation. Yearly increases in sales are significant only when these increases are reflected in the *bottom line*. This means that increases in sales *must be reflected in the earnings figures*. Gross inefficiencies in product quality have great impact on these earnings, and care must be exercised to determine if a company's earnings figures are increasing as a result of an accounting change *or* realized growth.

Footnotes in the Footnotes: A Tell-Tale Sign

Concentrate on the footnotes appended to the financial report. As a general rule, a large number of footnotes indicates that investors should closely examine the numbers. The footnotes can give clues about the quality of a company's earnings figures.

Examine the three key ratios: gross profit margin, operating profit margin, and net profit margin.

> *Growth profit margin.* The gross profit margin is equal to gross profit divided by net sales. This margin, when compared to other firms in the industry, indicates how the company can maintain and possibly expand its position within the industry.

> *Operating profit margin.* The operating profit margin is equal to operating profit divided by net sales; volatility of this figure is a good indication of radical swings and failure to maintain stable profits.

> *Net profit margin.* Divide net income by net sales to obtain the net profit margin, and compare this figure to industry norms to discover whether the company is *more* or *less* profitable than its competition.

How Do I Identify Income Stocks?

Identifying income stocks is complex and time-consuming and, in most cases, is best left to the experts since the novice is not sufficiently familiar with all the nuances of financial statements. Here is some insight. The weight given to financial "material" can vary enormously. As we hinted briefly, accounting methods can occlude the growth and profits picture. Similarly, the standing of investment-grade bonds and preferred stocks is controlled by the financial record. To identify income stocks, the analyst must concentrate on safety. The safety criterion varies with past earnings and so-called fixed charges (e.g., interest and preferred dividends). The dividend record, the relationship of the funded debt to the property account, the working capital position, and the actual *volume* of business all play critical roles in determining the "reliability" of income stock. The analysis criteria are explained in the following paragraphs.

Past Record

When common stocks are selected, much of the emphasis is placed on *future performance*. The separation of the future from the past can rarely occur in practice, however. Therefore the financial record becomes the only *tangible* basis for prediction. The statistical performance of common stock provides the only reliable indicator of future performance. Proper application of income statement and balance sheet analysis gives the *best* indication of where a stock is headed.

Patterns

Every company analysis has three major divisions: the capitalization, the record of earnings and dividends over a *significant* number of years, and a recent balance sheet. The recent balance sheet offers a discussion of the prospects of the business and the actual merits of the security. Without these analyses, it is difficult, if not impossible, to determine the *stability* of income.

The Prospectus

New security offerings provide elaborate, but incomplete, analytical studies called prospectuses. Although a prospectus contains a wealth of financial information for the past five years, it does not offer any pro and con discussions about the merits of the offering itself. The prospectus may carry a statement that indicates that the shares are "being offered as a speculation." This statement relieves the underwriters from possible liability for failure to indicate the presence of a substantial risk.

Brokerage-House Releases

Circulars issued by brokerage firms vary greatly in scope and competence. Some of these releases are not analyses, but are more accurately described as thinly disguised recommendations. There is usually a recommendation to buy.

Investment Service Reports

Larger investment services (e.g., Moody's, Standard & Poor's, and Value Line) offer condensed and analytical reports that will usually include a conclusion about the current attractiveness of the issue.

Income Statement

The more progressive analysts use the income statement as a guide for formulating estimates of future earnings or "earning power." Broad studies of corporate income statements are classified under the following aspects:

Accounting aspects. What are the true earnings over the period analyzed?

Business aspects. How does the earnings record show the future earning power of the company?

Security valuation. How does the analyst arrive at a *reasonable* valuation of the shares?

The combination of income analysis and balance sheet analysis forms the bulk of the "science" of predicting growth and, as you can see, is *not* fodder for any lightweight accountant.

It's review time.

QUESTIONS

Place the letter of the term next to the expression that best describes it.

A. Common stock
B. Proxy statement
C. Capital gains
D. Par value
E. Float
F. Treasury stock
G. Preferred stock
H. Cumulative preferred stock
I. Convertible preferred stock
J. Blue chip stock
K. Growth stock
L. Growth profit margin
M. Operating profit margin
N. Net profit margin
O. Past record
P. Prospectus
Q. Income account

_____ Dividends accumulate and become a debt of the company in the years in which the company is unable to pay a preferred dividend.

_____ Marked by high price and low yield.

_____ Helps the investor determine whether the company is more or less profitable than its competition.

_____ Analytical presentation of a new security offering.

_____ The most liquid form of individual investment.

_____ Used today only for bookkeeping purposes, for all practical purposes, this cannot be correlated to a stock's book value.

_____ Three key margins assess this type of stock.

_____ A good indication of radical swings and failure to maintain stable profits.

_____ The only tangible prediction of future performance.

_____ Supports the continuation of in-place management.

_____ Indicates how a company can maintain and possibly expand its position within the industry.

_____ With these stocks you have no voice in the selection of a company's officers and directors and no attractive alternatives to the acquisition of capital gains.

_____ Your ROI in stock price appreciation.

_____ Includes broad studies of the accounting aspects, security valuation, and business aspects of a company.

_____ Company reacquired stock.

_____ Has an option to convert to common stock.

_____ Number of shares outstanding minus the number of shares held by corporate insiders.

ANSWERS

H	K	C
J	M	Q
N	O	F
P	B	I
A	L	E
D	G	

PART II

Common Stock Valuation

Although breaking up is hard to do, it has been shown that some companies would be worth more *after* liquidating their assets and paying their debts than the price at which their shares can be traded on the open market. As long as the liquidation value is sufficiently high, corporate analysts must monitor the net liquidating value of a company (a value determined by dividing the liquidating value of the company by the number of shares outstanding) to see if this strategy is viable. This value may *not* be easily accessed by a quick look at the balance sheets. Although the estimation of breakup values takes up a hefty part of Wall Street analysts' time, most of the stock valuation processes are geared toward "going-concern" values.

Theorists of "present value" have had a long-term disagreement about the merits of expected future cash flows from investments versus their present market value. Investors are faced with the decision to either "take stock in" *potential* or *performance*.

There are three steps that all common stock investors must follow in making buying decisions:

1. Estimate the future earnings per share.
2. Estimate the proportion of earnings that is likely to be paid as dividends.
3. Calculate the present value of the projected dividend stream by discounting the dividends at the required rate of return (which reflects the actual degree of uncertainty about the overall accuracy of the estimates).

The experts express pros and cons about the ability to calculate a projected dividend stream—particularly when these calculations must be made into the distant future. It is recommended that *several* valuation methods be applied, and that investors attempt to find stocks with market prices that appear either low or high based on alternative estimates of their value. Three such valuations are presented for the reader's consideration:

1. Price/earnings ratios
2. Price/sales ratios
3. Price/book value ratios

Present Value Mathematics[1]

The Basic Concept

The concept of present value is really quite simple and can be easily illustrated. Assume that Mr. A wants to borrow money from Ms. B, repayable at a future date. Ms. B is willing to grant the loan but feels that, considering the risks involved, she is entitled to a 10 percent annual rate of return. This being the case, how much money will B advance to A on A's IOU for $1,000 payable one year hence? The answer is $909.09. If B lends $909.09 and gets back $1,000.00 a year later, she has earned $90.91 in interest during the year ($1,000–$909.09), which is 10 percent of the amount loaned. Thus, $909.09 is the present value of $1,000 payable 1 year hence at a discount rate of 10 percent (in present value calculations, the interest rate is known as the discount rate). Algebraically, the relationships in this example can be described in two ways:

1. Future value = Present value × (1 + Interest rate)
   $1,000.00 = $909.09   × 1.10
2. Present value = Future value /(1 + Interest rate)
   $909.09   = $1,000.00   /1.10

Suppose, now, that the $1,000 IOU was to be payable 2 years hence instead of 1 year hence. If B still wants a 10 percent per annum rate of return, she would be willing to lend $826.45. This can be seen as follows:

Year   1: × 1.10 = $909.09 ($826.45 + $82.64)
$826.45
Year   2: × 1.10 = $1,000.00 ($909.09 + $90.91)
$909.09

As a generalization, we can state that:

$$\text{Future value} = \text{Present value} \times (1 + i)^n$$
$$\text{Present value} = \text{Future value}/(1 + i)^n$$

---

[1]SOURCE *Investment Analyses and Portfolio Management,* New York Institute of Finance, New York, NY, 1987.

where:

i = annual compound interest rate or discount rate (compounding means that interest is to be earned not only on the initial principal amount but also on each interest payment)

n = number of years between the present and the future value

We can further generalize for cases where interest is to be compounded more frequently than once a year. For example, bonds usually pay interest twice a year, stocks usually pay dividends quarterly, and many savings banks compound interest daily. The more generalized formulas would be:

$$\text{Future value} = \text{Present value} \times [1 + (i + (i/m)]^{mn}$$
$$\text{Present value} = \text{Future value}/[1 + (i/m)]^{mn}$$

where

i = stated, or nominal annual interest or discount rate

m = number of compounding periods each year

n = number of years between present and future value

Present and Future Value Tables

In order to simplify such calculations, tables have been developed for the future value of $1 and the present value of $1.[2] Tables 5.1 and 5.2 are typical. Note that each column represents a different interest rate, and each row represents a different number of compounding periods. To illustrate the use of these tables, consider the following questions:

1. If you borrow $5,000 and promise to repay the loan after 5 years, with interest at 10 percent, compounded annually, how much will you have to repay?
2. If you promise to pay me $5,000 after 10 years, how much should I be willing to lend you today if I demand 12 percent interest, compounded annually?
3. Suppose, in question 2, that I demand 12 percent compounded quarterly?

[2]Most good handheld calculators will also do the job conveniently.

To answer question 1, to to Table 5.1. Run your finger down to the row for period 5 and across to the 10 percent column. You will find the number 1.6105. This means that the future value of $1 after 5 years, at 10 percent compounded annually, is $1.6105. Since the loan is $5,000, multiply $5,000 by 1.6105, and the answer is that you will have to repay $8,052.50.

To answer question 2, go to Table 5.2. Run your finger down to the row for period 10 and across to the 12 percent column. You will find the number .3220. This means that the present value of $1 payable 10 years from now is only 32 cents, at a 12 percent annual discount rate. Since you promise to pay me $5,000 in 10 years, I will lend you $1,610 ($5,000 × .3220).

TABLE 5.1   Future Value of $1 Payable at End of N Periods

N	1%	2%	3%	4%	5%	6%	7%	8%	9%	10%	12%	14%	15%	16%	18%	20%
1	1.0100	1.0200	1.0300	1.0400	1.0500	1.0600	1.0700	1.0800	1.0900	1.1000	1.1200	1.1400	1.1500	1.1600	1.1800	1.2000
2	1.0201	1.0404	1.0609	1.0816	1.1025	1.1236	1.1449	1.1664	1.1881	1.2100	1.2544	1.2996	1.3225	1.3456	1.3924	1.4400
3	1.0303	1.0612	1.0927	1.1249	1.1576	1.1910	1.2250	1.2597	1.2950	1.3310	1.4049	1.4815	1.5209	1.5609	1.6430	1.7280
4	1.0406	1.0824	1.1255	1.1699	1.2155	1.2625	1.3108	1.3905	1.4116	1.4641	1.5735	1.6890	1.7490	1.8106	1.9388	2.0736
5	1.0510	1.1041	1.1593	1.2167	1.2763	1.3382	1.4026	1.4693	1.5386	1.6105	1.7623	1.9254	2.0114	2.1003	2.2878	2.4883
6	1.0615	1.1262	1.1941	1.2653	1.3401	1.4185	1.5007	1.5869	1.6771	1.7716	1.9738	2.1950	2.3131	2.4364	2.6996	2.9800
7	1.0721	1.1487	1.2299	1.3159	1.4071	1.5036	1.6058	1.7138	1.8280	1.9487	2.2107	2.5023	2.6600	2.8262	3.1855	3.5832
8	1.0829	1.1717	1.2668	1.3686	1.4775	1.5938	1.7182	1.8509	1.9926	2.1436	2.4760	2.8526	3.0590	3.2784	3.7589	4.2998
9	1.0937	1.1951	1.3048	1.4233	1.5513	1.6895	1.8385	1.9990	2.1719	2.3579	2.7731	3.2519	3.5179	3.8030	4.4355	5.1598
10	1.1046	1.2190	1.3439	1.4802	1.6289	1.7908	1.9672	2.1589	2.3674	2.5937	3.1058	3.7072	4.0456	4.4114	5.2338	6.1917
11	1.1157	1.2434	1.3842	1.5395	1.7103	1.8983	2.1049	2.3316	2.5804	2.8531	3.4785	4.2262	4.6524	5.1173	6.1759	7.4301
12	1.1268	1.2682	1.4258	1.6010	1.7959	2.0122	2.2522	2.5182	2.8127	3.1384	3.8960	4.8179	5.3502	5.9360	7.2876	8.9161
13	1.1381	1.2936	1.4685	1.6651	1.8856	2.1329	2.4093	2.7196	3.0658	3.4523	4.3635	5.4924	6.1528	6.8858	8.5994	10.699
14	1.1495	1.3195	1.5126	1.7317	1.9799	2.2609	2.5785	2.3372	3.3417	3.7975	4.8871	6.2613	7.0757	7.9875	10.147	12.839
15	1.1610	1.3459	1.5580	1.8009	2.0789	2.3966	2.7590	2.1722	3.6425	4.1772	5.4736	7.1379	8.1371	9.2655	11.973	15.407
16	1.1726	1.3728	1.6047	1.8730	2.1829	2.5404	2.9522	3.4259	3.9703	4.5950	6.1304	8.1372	9.3576	10.748	14.129	18.488
17	1.1843	1.4002	1.6528	1.9479	2.2920	2.6928	3.1588	3.7000	4.3276	5.0545	6.8660	9.2765	10.761	12.467	16.672	22.186
18	1.1961	1.4282	1.7024	2.0258	2.4066	2.8543	3.3799	3.9960	4.7171	5.5599	7.6900	10.575	12.375	14.462	19.673	26.623
19	1.2081	1.4568	1.7535	2.1068	2.5270	3.0256	3.6165	4.3157	5.1417	6.1159	8.6128	12.055	14.231	16.776	23.214	31.948
20	1.2202	1.4859	1.8061	2.1911	2.6533	3.2071	3.8697	4.6610	5.6044	6.7275	9.6463	13.743	16.366	19.460	27.393	38.337
25	1.2824	1.6406	2.0938	2.6658	3.3864	4.2919	5.4274	6.8485	8.6231	10.834	17.000	26.461	32.918	40.874	62.668	95.396
30	1.3478	1.8114	2.4273	3.2434	4.3219	5.7435	7.6123	10.062	13.267	17.449	29.959	50.950	66.211	85.849	143.37	237.37
40	1.4889	2.2080	3.2620	4.8010	7.0400	10.285	14.974	21.724	31.409	45.259	93.050	188.88	267.86	378.72	750.37	1469.7
50	1.6446	2.6916	4.3839	7.1067	11.467	18.420	29.457	46.901	74.357	117.39	289.00	700.23	1083.6	1670.7	3927.3	9100.4
60	1.8167	3.2810	5.8916	10.519	18.679	32.987	57.946	101.25	176.03	304.48	897.59	2595.9	4383.9	7370.1	20555.	56347.

TABLE 5.2   Present Value of $1 Payable at End of *N* Periods

N	1%	2%	3%	4%	5%	6%	7%	8%	9%	10%	12%	14%	15%	16%	18%	20%
1	.9901	.9804	.9709	.9615	.9524	.9434	.9346	.9259	.9174	.9091	.8929	.8772	.8696	.8621	.8475	.8333
2	.9803	.9612	.9426	.9246	.9070	.8900	.8734	.8573	.8417	.8264	.7972	.7695	.7561	.7432	.7182	.6944
3	.9706	.9423	.9151	.8890	.8638	.8396	.8163	.7938	.7722	.7513	.7118	.6750	.6575	.6407	.6086	.5787
4	.9610	.9238	.8885	.8548	.8227	.7921	.7629	.7350	.7084	.6830	.6355	.5921	.5718	.5523	.5158	.4823
5	.9515	.9057	.8626	.8219	.7835	.7473	.7130	.6806	.6499	.6209	.5674	.5194	.4972	.4761	.4371	.4019
6	.9420	.8880	.8375	.7903	.7462	.7050	.6663	.6302	.5963	.5645	.5066	.4556	.4323	.4104	.3704	.3349
7	.9327	.8706	.8131	.7599	.7107	.6651	.6227	.5835	.5470	.5132	.4523	.3996	.3759	.3538	.3139	.2791
8	.9235	.8535	.7894	.7307	.6768	.6274	.5820	.5463	.5019	.4665	.4039	.3506	.3269	.3050	.2660	.2326
9	.9143	.8368	.7664	.7026	.6446	.5919	.5439	.5002	.4604	.4241	.3606	.3075	.2843	.2630	.2255	.1938
10	.9053	.8203	.7441	.6756	.6139	.5584	.5083	.4632	.4224	.3855	.3220	.2697	.2472	.2267	.1911	.1615
11	.8963	.8643	.7224	.6496	.5847	.5268	.4751	.4289	.3875	.3505	.2875	.2366	.2149	.1954	.1619	.1346
12	.8874	.7885	.7014	.6246	.5568	.4970	.4440	.3971	.3555	.3186	.2567	.2076	.1869	.1685	.1372	.1122
13	.8787	.7730	.6810	.6006	.5303	.4688	.4150	.3677	.3262	.2897	.2292	.1821	.1625	.1452	.1163	.0935
14	.8700	.7579	.6611	.5775	.5051	.4423	.3878	.3405	.2992	.2633	.2046	.1597	.1413	.1252	.0385	.0779
15	.8613	.7430	.6419	.5553	.4810	.4173	.3624	.3152	.2745	.2394	.1827	.1401	.1229	.1079	.0335	.0649
16	.8528	.7284	.6232	.5339	.4581	.3936	.3387	.2919	.2519	.2176	.1631	.1229	.1069	.0930	.0708	.0541
17	.8444	.7142	.6050	.5134	.4383	.3714	.3166	.2703	.2311	.1978	.1456	.1078	.0929	.0802	.0600	.0451
18	.8360	.7002	.5874	.4936	.4155	.3503	.2959	.2502	.2120	.1799	.1300	.0946	.0808	.0631	.0508	.0376
19	.8277	.6864	.5703	.4746	.3957	.3305	.2765	.2317	.1945	.1635	.1161	.0829	.0703	.0596	.0431	.0313
20	.8195	.6730	.5537	.4564	.3769	.3118	.2584	.2145	.1784	.1486	.1037	.0728	.0611	.0514	.0365	.0261
25	.7798	.6095	.4776	.3751	.2953	.2330	.1842	.1460	.1160	.0923	.0588	.0378	.0304	.0245	.0160	.0105
30	.7419	.5521	.4120	.3083	.2314	.1741	.1314	.0994	.0754	.0573	.0334	.0196	.0151	.0116	.0070	.0042
40	.6717	.4529	.3066	.2083	.1420	.0972	.0668	.0460	.0318	.0221	.0107	.0053	.0037	.0026	.0013	.0007
50	.6080	.3715	.2281	.1407	.0572	.0543	.0339	.0213	.0134	.0085	.0035	.0014	.0009	.0006	.0003	.0001
60	.5504	.3048	.1697	.0951	.0535	.0303	.0173	.0699	.0057	.0033	.0011	.0004	.0002	.0001	.0000	.0000

To answer question 3, stay at Table 5.2 but go to the 40-period row (10 years, compounded quarterly) and the 3 percent interest rate column (12 percent payable quarterly is 3 percent per quarter). The number is .3066. In this example, therefore, I would lend you $1,533 ($5,000 × .3066).

Spend some time perusing Tables 5.1 and 5.2, and you will see why Albert Einstein described compound interest as man's greatest invention. At fairly low interest rates, the future value of $1 does not rise very rapidly as the number of periods increases. But as the interest rate gets higher, a dollar grows to staggering amounts with the passage of time. By the same token, a dollar payable many years from now is worth very little today at high discount rates such as have been common in recent years.

Dividend Discount Models[3]

The concept that a common stock is worth the present value of future dividends is expressed in the following equation:

$$P_o = \frac{d_1}{(1 + k)} + \frac{d_2}{(1 + k)^2} + \cdots \frac{d_n}{(1 + k)^n}$$

$$= \sum_{t=1}^{\infty} \frac{d_t}{(1 + k)^t}$$

where

P_o = the worth of the stock today

$d_1, d_2 \ldots d_n$ = the expected annual dividend stream

k = the discount rate (rate of return) deemed appropriate for the uncertainty of the dividend estimates (annual compounding will be assumed in this and all subsequent calculations in this chapter)

From this generalized statement, three types of dividend streams can be considered:

1. Dividends are expected to remain unchanged.
2. Dividends are expected to grow at a constant rate (g). (We will not deal with declining dividend streams, but the basic mathematics would not be different.)
3. Dividends are expected to grow at a variable rate $(g_1, g_2 \ldots)$

Similarly, the discount rate (k) can be assumed to remain constant or to change over time. Within the framework of the Capital Asset Pricing Model, the discount rate would reflect the magnitude of: (a) the risk-free rate, (b) the risk premium of stocks as an asset class versus risk-free assets, and (c) any additional uncertainties inherent in forecasting the cash flows of the particular stock.

---

[3]SOURCE *Investment Analyses and Portfolio Management*, New York Institute of Finance, New York, NY, 1987.

The Zero Growth Model

If dividends are expected to remain unchanged at today's rate (d_o), and the discount rate also is expected to remain constant, the basic valuation equation reduces to:

$$P_o = \frac{d_o}{k}$$

This formula is applicable only to the valuation of preferred stocks, which have fixed dividend rates, or to the common stocks of very mature companies such as big-city electric utilities, whose dividends are likely to show little, if any, secular growth. As the formula indicates, such stocks are evaluated by dividing the indicated dividend rate (d_o) by an appropriate dividend yield (k). The appropriate yield usually is derived from the recent relationship between the yield on the particular stock and the yield on high-grade bonds. For example, the stocks of mature electric utilities usually sell at prices which provide dividend yields approximately equal to U.S. Treasury bond yields. Therefore, they may be considered undervalued ("cheap") when their dividend yields exceed Treasury bond yields and overvalued ("expensive") when their dividend yields are below Treasury bond yields.[4]

The Constant Growth Model

If dividends are expected to grow at a constant rate (g), the stream of dividends will be: $d_o(1 + g), d_o(1 + g)^2 \ldots d_o(1 + g)^x$. Assuming a constant discount rate (k), the basic valuation formula would be:

---

[4]Strictly speaking, there is an implication that some dividend growth is expected. Otherwise, the dividend yield on a utility stock should exceed the yield on a Treasury bond since the latter has no default risk while the former has a risk of declining dividends if not outright bankruptcy. Preferred stock dividend yields, interestingly, usually are *below* high-grade bond yields; but this is because their income is largely tax-exempt to corporate buyers. On a "taxable-equivalent" basis, preferred stock yields are higher than bond yields.

$$P_o = \frac{d_0(1 + g)}{(1 + k)} + \frac{d_0(1 + g)^2}{(1 + k)^2} + \dots \frac{d_0(1 + g)^\infty}{(1 + k)^\infty}$$

$$= \sum_{t=1}^{\infty} \frac{d_0(1 + g)^t}{(1 + k)^t}$$

As long as it is assumed that k is greater than g (a reasonable assumption since a continuous growth rate in excess of the discount rate would produce an infinite present value), the equation can be simplified to:[5]

$$P_o = \frac{d_1}{(k - g)}$$

This formula is most applicable to the valuation of the overall market (as represented by, say, the Standard & Poor's 500 Composite Stock Price Index) or of very large, broadly diversified companies. In these cases, it is possible to envision growth extending over a great number of years at a rate which can be described as constant despite the presence of cyclical fluctuations around the underlying trend.

A simple transformation of the formula gives it another interesting property. Since

$$P_o = \frac{d_1}{(k - g)} \qquad \text{then} \qquad (k - g) = \frac{d_1}{(P_o)}$$

Therefore, $(k - g)$ can be viewed as a normalized dividend yield. That is, given assumptions about k and g, a constant growth stock or group of stocks would be considered fairly valued at a price that produces a dividend yield equal to k minus g.

Furthermore, it can be seen that:

[5]For a mathematical proof of this simplification, together with an extensive discussion of other valuation formulas, see J. Fred Weston and Eugene F. Brigham, *Essentials of Managerial Finance,* 5th ed. (Hinsdale, Ill.: Dryden Press, 1979), Chapter 14.

$$k = \frac{d_1}{P_o} + g$$

From this expression, it follows that an investor who has an idea about the likely constant dividend growth rate of a stock can estimate the total rate of return that will be produced from a purchase by adding the estimated growth rate to the first year's dividend yield. For example, a dividend yield of 6 percent and a long-term growth rate of 6 percent will produce a *long-term* total return of 12 percent.[6]

Constant Growth Model Applied to the Overall Market

In July 1985, the S&P 500 Index reached a new record high in excess of 190, having gained about 90 percent from the level to which it had fallen 3 years earlier during a cyclical downturn. For an investor trying to determine the reasonableness of the new high price level of the market, the constant growth dividend discount model ($P_o = d_1/(k - g)$) might have been quite helpful.

At the time the S&P Index reached its new high, the majority view of economists regarding the long-term economic outlook was that real GNP would grow at a rate of about 3 percent (consisting of about $1\frac{1}{2}$ percent growth rate in employment and $1\frac{1}{2}$ percent productivity growth) and that inflation would average about 6 percent, for total long-term GNP growth of about 9 percent per annum.[7] Since corporate sales, earnings, and dividends had grown more slowly than GNP for many years,[8] an investor in mid-1985 might reasonably have forecast long-term dividend growth (g) at a rate of about 8

---

[6]Emphasis is placed on the words *long-term*. If the stock is purchased at a dividend yield of 6 percent and sold a couple of years later at a substantially lower (or higher) dividend yield, the total return for the holding period will be quite different from 12 percent.

[7]See, for example, Alan Murray, "Extent of Future U.S. Growth," *The Wall Street Journal*, December 13, 1984.

[8]For a good analysis, see Dale N. Allman, "The Decline in Business Profitability," *Economic Review of the Federal Reserve Bank of Kansas City*, January 1983.

Dividends grew even more slowly than earnings mainly because, in an inflationary environment, the replacement cost of plant and equipment rose faster than internal cash generation, so that a shrinkage of dividend payout ratios, along with an increase in debt, was needed to finance capital outlays.

percent per annum versus 9 percent for GNP. This same investor, had he or she been a student of history, would have known that the stock market had produced a real rate of return (i.e., net of inflation) of about 7 percent over extended time periods.[9] Therefore, with a 6 percent inflation rate, a reasonable rate at which to discount corporate dividends (k) might be about 13 percent. Finally, the investor would have noted that in mid-1985, dividends on the S&P 500 Index were running at a rate of almost 8.00.[10] Therefore, the trend rate of dividends a year forward (d_1) might be about 8.50.

Substituting these variables in the valuation equation, ($P_o = d_1 / (k - g)$), the investor might have concluded that the intrinsic value of the S&P 500 Index in mid-1985 was: 8.50/(.13 − .08), or about 170. At an actual price level of over 190, the stock market might have appeared to be a bit high relative to long-term economic prospects.

On the other hand, our investor might have focused on two nonconventional views of the economic outlook. One nonconventional view, associated with supply-side economists, was that incentive-oriented fiscal and monetary policies would increase productivity, real GNP, and corporate profitability without aggravating inflation. According to this view, dividend growth (g) would be about 10 percent per annum, so that the value of the S&P 500 Index would be approximately: 8.50/(.13 − .10), or 283, and the market could rise a great deal further before becoming overpriced. But another nonconventional view, the "stagflation school," was that continuing huge federal deficits would sap much of the vitality of the private economy and lead to much higher rates of inflation. This view might have put real GNP growth at only 2½ percent, inflation at over 9 percent, total GNP growth at 12 percent, dividend growth at 10 percent, and the common stock discount rate at 16 percent. The value of the S&P 500 Index would be approximately: 8.50/(.16 − .10), or 142, thus posing serious downside risk from the 190 level of mid-1985.

The various views could be summarized as in Table 5.3, with sample probabilities assigned to each. The conclusion would prob-

---

[9]The most widely quoted study of historical asset returns has been Roger G. Ibbotson and Rex A. Sinqfield, *Stocks, Bonds, Bills and Inflation: The Past and The Future*, Financial Analysts Research Foundation, Charlottesville, Va., 1982).

[10]Data on the index are published by Standard & Poor's in *The Analysts Handbook*.

TABLE 5.3   Hypothetical Valuation Criteria For S&P 500 Index in Mid-1985

Viewpoint	Inflation	Dividend Growth (g)	Discount Rate (k)	Normalized Dividend Yield (k − g)	S&P Value*	Subjective Probability
Consensus	6%	8%	13%	5%	170	.5
Supply-side	6	10	13	3	283	.3
Stagflation	9	10	16	6	142	.2
Probability-weighted average†	6½	9	13½	4½	198	

*These values assume that the normalized dividend level one year forward (d_1) was 8.50 in all three cases, which would not be quite correct but seems adequate for exposition purposes.
†For simplicity, the weighted averages are expressed in round numbers.

ably have been that the market was fairly priced even at its record high level.[11]

The Variable Growth Model

While continuous growth in excess of the discount rate ($g > k$) is an unreasonable assumption because it produces infinite present values, many companies do exhibit very rapid growth for 5, 10, or more

[11]It will be noted in the table that different assumptions regarding k and g, in different economic environments, produce different normalized dividend yields ($k − g$). There is, however, a body of theory which argues that ($k − g$) should be a constant, at least in the long run. The argument is that the major factor causing changes in k is changes in the expected rate of inflation; but changes in expected inflation, it is claimed, should equally impact the expected growth rate of earnings and dividends (g) since corporations tend to pass on inflationary and disinflationary forces to their customers. Much of the argument contends that measured profits during inflation do not account for the real economic profits that accrue from a reduction in real corporate liabilities. These views have been presented forcefully in Franco Modigliani and Richard A. Cohn, "Inflation, Rational Valuation and the Market," *Financial Analysts Journal*, March–April 1979; and in Burton Malkiel, *The Inflation-Beater's Investment Guide* (New York: W. W. Norton, 1980). Not only does the empirical evidence tend to contradict these theoretical arguments, the theory itself has some deficiencies, as described by Martin Feldstein in "Inflation and the Stock Market," *American Economic Review*, December 1980. On the other hand, there is some evidence that the "inflation passthrough" argument may apply to assets like commercial real estate. See Leon G. Cooperman, Steven G. Einhorn, and Meyer Melnikoff, *The Case for Pension Fund Investment in Property*, Goldman Sachs, New York, 1983).

years. Ultimately, usually as a result of product obsolescence or competition, the growth slows. Indeed, if it did not, the company would eventually swallow up the entire economy. Analysts deal with such cases by assuming that growth will pass through one or more stages of deceleration until finally settling down at a constant growth rate equal to that of the average company. The constant growth formula is applied to determine the value of the stock at that point, and that assumed terminal price is discounted to the present and added to the present value of the dividends paid during the rapid-growth period. That is:

$$P_o = \text{Present value of dividends prior to constant growth period}$$
$$\text{plus}$$
$$\text{Present value of assumed terminal price of stock}$$

Illustration

Suppose that we were trying to place a value on the stock of Texas Instruments in July 1985. The price of the stock was about $100 per share, having ranged from $150 to $90 during the prior 18 months. The dividend rate was $2.00 per share compared with cyclically volatile earnings that had averaged about $5.50 per share over a 5-year period.

Suppose we assumed that Texas Instruments' future growth would pass through two stages. The first stage would be a 10-year period in which earnings per share grew at a fairly rapid rate, somewhat in excess of 15 percent, and dividends grew at an even more rapid 20 percent, having started at a relatively low level. The second stage would see growth permanently stabilized at an average of about 10 percent.

Thus:

$$g_1 = 20 \text{ percent and lasts for 10 years } (n = 10)$$
$$g_2 = 10 \text{ percent and persists thereafter}$$

Further, suppose we assume that an appropriate discount rate for this stock is 14 percent, except that the uncertainty of the forecast of

an extra-rapid growth rate for the first 10 years suggests a larger discount rate during that period, perhaps 18 percent.
Thus:

$$k_1 = 18\%; \; k_2 = 14\%$$

The value of Texas Instruments' stock in this example would be somewhat under $90 per share, derived as shown in the equation and Table 5.4 below. If the assumptions underlying this valuation were approximately correct, the stock's price of $100 per share in July 1985 was reasonable, being fairly close to its intrinsic value. But at the earlier high of $150, the stock was substantially overpriced.

$$P_o = \left[\sum_{t=1}^{n} \frac{d_o(1 + g_1)^t}{(1 + k_1)^t} \right] + \left[\frac{d_{n+1}}{(k_2 - g_2)} \times \frac{1}{(1 + k_1)^n} \right]$$

$$= \left[\sum_{t=1}^{10} \frac{2.00(1.20)^t}{(1.18)^t} \right] + \left[\frac{d_{11}}{(.14 - .10)} \times \frac{1}{(1.18)^{10}} \right]$$

$$= \$21.96 + \$65.08$$

$$= \$87.04$$

Three-Stage Variable Growth Models

The Texas Instruments illustration, just presented, assumed a sudden change in the 11th year from a rapid 20 percent growth rate to an average 10 percent growth rate. However, many security analysts who employ dividend discount models consider it more realistic to assume that above-average growth rates gravitate toward average in a more gradual, three-stage fashion. This is illustrated in Figure 5.1, which shows the earnings and dividends stream of a company that grows rapidly and then gradually slows down.

Utilizing this framework, computer programs have been developed which call for specification of the following variables:

TABLE 5.4   Two-Stage Growth Valuation

1. Present Value of Dividends During Initial Growth Period (20 percent annual growth for 10 years, discounted at 18 percent annual rate)

Period (n)	(1) Value of Dividends (d_t) (See Table 5.1)	(2) Present Value Factor (See Table 5.2)	Present Value of Dividends (Columns 1 × 2)
0	$ 2.0000	—	—
1	2.4000	.8475	$ 2.0340
2	2.8800	.7182	2.0684
3	3.4560	.6086	2.1034
4	4.1472	.5158	2.1392
5	4.9766	.4371	2.1752
6	5.9720	.3704	2.2120
7	7.1664	.3139	2.2496
8	8.5996	.2660	2.2874
9	10.3196	.2255	2.3270
10	12.3834	.1911	2.3664
			$21.9626

$$\sum_{t=1}^{10} \frac{2.00(1.20)^t}{(1.18)^t} = \$21.9626$$

2. Present Value of Assumed Terminal Price

$$\frac{d_{11}}{k_2 - g_2} = \frac{\$12.3834 \times 1.10}{.14 - .10} = \frac{\$13.6215}{.04} = \$340.54$$

$$\frac{1}{(1 + k_1)^{10}} = \frac{1}{(1.18)^{10}} = \frac{1}{5.2338} \qquad = .1911^*$$

$$\$340.54 \times .1911 = \$65.08$$

*See Table 5.2 for verification.

FIGURE 5.1   The Three-Stage Growth Framework

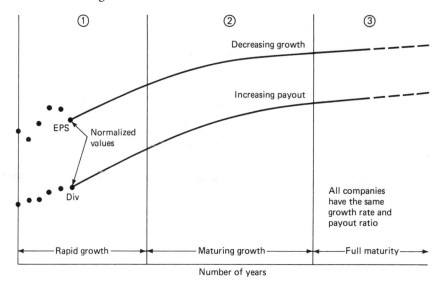

SOURCE   Drexel Burnham Lambert.

1. Normalized earnings and dividends for the current year—that
   is, the earnings and dividends that would likely prevail if the
   business environment were neither cyclically high nor low.
2. The number of years in stage 1—that is, the number of years
   during which the analyst can confidently forecast that the
   company will exhibit well-above-average earnings growth.
3. The specific earnings growth rate expected during stage 1.
4. The dividend payout ratio expected by the end of stage 1. (The
   first year's payout ratio is implied by the normalized dividends
   and earnings per share specified for the current year.)
5. The number of years in stage 2—that is, the period during
   which the earnings growth rate will decelerate toward the
   average growth rate and during which the payout ratio will
   rise toward the average payout ratio.
6. Whether the growth rate and payout ratio transition in stage 2
   will proceed in a straight line or curvilinear manner. (Figure
   5.1 assumes a curvilinear transition path. Actually, if the
   transition period is 10 or more years, both linear and curvilinear assumptions produce fairly similar results.)
7. Stage 3—that is, the "forever after"—earnings growth rate
   and payout ratio.

Given this information, the computer calculates each year's dividends up to the point where constant growth to infinity is assumed. At this point, dividend valuation computer programs differ considerably in complexity. In the simplest case, the current price of the stock is specified, and the computer calculates the discount rate which equates the stream of dividends with the current price. This "implied discount rate" is the rate of return which will be earned by an investor who buys at the current price and holds "forever," assuming that the growth rate, payout, and time period assumptions are correct. The investor can then decide if this rate of return is greater or less than he or she requires for the risks involved, in which case the stock is either considered underpriced or overpriced.

Most sophisticated computer programs go beyond merely calculating the implied discount rate. They rely on the capital asset pricing equation, which specifies that the expected rate of return for a stock (R_s) is a function of the risk-free rate (R_f), the rate of return expected for the market in aggregate (R_m), and the stock's systematic risk, or beta (B). Specifically, the user specifies R_f, R_m, and B, in the equation $R_s = R_f + B (R_m - R_f)$, and the computer calculates R_s, which can be called the required discount rate.[12] The required discount rate is then compared with the implied discount rate and the degree of over- or underpricing is expressed as a positive or negative risk-adjusted excess return, referred to as *alpha* in portfolio theory.

For example, suppose the current price of a stock equates with the expected dividend stream at an implied discount rate of 17.4 percent, while the capital asset pricing equation suggests a required rate (risk-adjusted) of 16.2 percent. The computer will show that purchase of the stock will produce an annualized risk-adjusted excess return, or alpha, of +1.2 percent. This can be done for every stock being analyzed, and the computer can print out a listing of all the stocks ranked from the most positive to the most negative alpha.

[12]Some models assume there is a capital market *plane* rather than a *line*, in which R_s is also, in part, a function of the stock's relative dividend yield. The reason for taking dividend yield explicitly into account is that the component of R_s which comes from current income has usually been taxed at a different rate than the component which comes from growth. See William M. Bethke and Susan E. Boyd, "Should Dividend Models be Yield-Titled?" *Journal of Portfolio Management*, Spring 1983.

For a description of how to program a dividend discount model on a hand-held programmable computer see Russell J. Fuller, "Programming the Three-Phase Dividend Discount Model," *Journal of Portfolio Management*, Summer 1979.

Another version of the same basic approach is for the computer, after calculating the required discount rate, to then discount the dividend stream at that rate and derive an intrinsic present value. The current stock price can then be compared with this intrinsic value, and a percentage over- or underpricing is calculated. Using the previous example, suppose that the intrinsic value at the required 16.2 percent discount rate is $50 per share.[13] And suppose the current price (with an implied discount rate of 17.4 percent) is $40 per share. The price/value ratio is 40/50, or 80 percent. A similar ratio can be calculated for every stock being analyzed, and a list can be produced which ranks the stocks from lowest (most undervalued) to highest (most overvalued) price/value ratio.[14]

Illustrations

Many brokerage firms offer their institutional clients monthly valuation tabulations and graphs derived from computer programs such as we have been describing, and many financial institutions have developed their own in-house versions.[15]

One of the more creative formats for presenting valuation data is published by Morgan Stanley. In addition to providing its clients with valuations for individual stocks, Morgan Stanley attempts to see if there are any mispricings of broad groupings of stocks. Charts show the relationships, at different points of time, between the price/value ratios produced by the Morgan Stanley model and expected growth rates, betas, quality ratings (Morgan Stanley classifies stocks into six quality categories), and company size (they have 10 size groups ranging from largest to smallest capitalization).

Figure 5.2, for example, focuses on the relationship between

---

[13]In this illustration, the required discount rate is derived using the stock's current beta value. Some computer programs take account of the likelihood that if the character of the company's growth does, indeed, change from its present path to that of the average company, the stock's beta will gradually converge toward 1.0. These programs, in effect, use a different required discount rate at each stage of growth to calculate the intrinsic value, and the overall required return is a weighted average of the returns in each stage.

[14]There is not a precise mathematical correspondence between excess return and price/value ratio. That is, two stocks may both have excess returns of 1.2 percent but different price/value ratios. However, the *ranking* of stocks tends to be fairly similar using both measures.

[15]See Barbara Donnelly, "The Dividend Discount Model Comes into Its Own," *Institutional Investor*, March 1985.

value and quality at two points in time—July 1985 (solid line) and June 1973 (dashed line). Both time periods, in Morgan Stanley's view, were characterized by slow economic growth and disinflation. The chart shows that in July 1985 higher-quality stocks were undervalued relative to lower-quality stocks whereas the reverse was true in the earlier period. Morgan Stanley highlighted this difference because, in their opinion, the earlier relationship was more representative of what the value-versus-quality relationship should be in a slow-growth, disinflationary economic environment. Therefore, they recommended that their clients switch out of lower-quality stocks and into higher-quality issues in order to benefit from the change in valuations that they expected to take place.

As another illustration of the usefulness of dividend discount models, consider Figure 5.3. This chart tracks the performance of a simple three-stage model applied to the largest 250 stocks in the S&P 500 Index over a 12-year period. Each year, the 250 stocks are divided into quintiles from lowest to highest rate of return implicit in the beginning-of-year market prices of the stocks (given consensus expectations regarding each of their dividend growth patterns.) The cumulative wealth actually produced by one dollar invested in the top two and bottom two quintiles at the start of the period is shown

FIGURE 5.2   Quality Rating and Relative Value (Equally Weighted Averages)

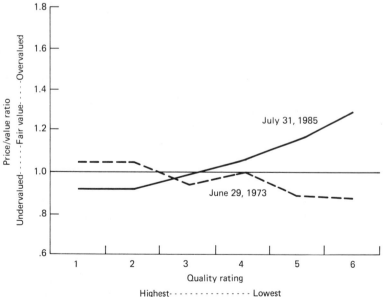

SOURCE   Morgan Stanley, *Investment Perspectives*, August 27, 1985.

FIGURE 5.3   Cumulative Wealth Derived from $1 Invested in 1972 (Discounted Dividend Valuation Quintiles versus S&P 500 Index)

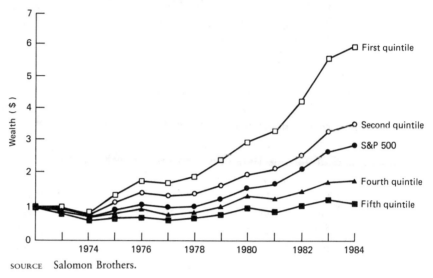

SOURCE   Salomon Brothers.

in the chart, along with the cumulative wealth produced by the S&P 500 Index. Note that the two top-ranked quintiles produced remarkably good results, while the lowest-ranked quintiles underperformed the overall market.

Complications

Despite its proven usefulness, many professional investors shy away from the dividend discount framework of analysis because of a number of inherent complexities. First, it is recognized that assumptions about corporate developments in stage 3 (15 or more years in the future) are extremely tenuous. Second, even small differences in key assumptions regarding stages 1 and 2 produce large differences in calculated intrinsic values.[16] Finally, many rapidly growing companies pay little or no dividends, and speculation on when such payments will begin is felt to be futile.

[16]For example, in a model that has been utilized by the Prudential Insurance Company, every change of one percentage point of growth assumed in stage 1 produces, on average, a change of 10 percent in intrinsic value. A change in assumed beta of .15 produces, on average, a 10 percent change in value. Similar alterations in value occur from changes in assumptions about the time span of stage 1 or stage 2.

Price/Earnings Ratios

Dividend discount models are complex and have a low level of proven usefulness. Most people who practice securities analysis continue to use the less sophisticated price/earnings ratios (P/E ratios). We shall not attempt to explain the mathematics of the P/E ratio beyond that already covered in our presentation in Chapter 4. Examine for a minute the table of the P/E ratio of the *Standard & Poor's 500 Composite Stock Price Index* in Table 5.5.

The P/E earnings ratio seems to follow these economic and investment trends:

P/E Ratio Range	Trend
7 to 9	Investors as a *group* are fearful of an economic depression or rampant inflation.
10 to 14	Investors experience a market that is oscillating between fear and confidence.
15 to 18	Investors look to the future with confidence.

TABLE 5.5 **P/E Ratio of Standard & Poor's 500 Composite Stock Price Index**

Year	P/E Ratio	Year	P/E Ratio	Year	P/E Ratio
1948	7	1960	17	1973	13
1949	7	1961	21	1974	9
1950	6	1962	17	1975	11
1951	9	1963	17	1976	10
1952	10	1964	18	1977	9
1953	10	1965	17	1978	8
1954	11	1966	15	1979	7
1955	11	1967	17	1980	8
1956	14	1968	17	1981	8
1957	13	1969	17	1982	9
1958	16	1970	16	1983	12
1959	17	1971	17	1984	10
		1972	17	1985	12

These are empirical generalizations that surprisingly hold to the *history* that supports them.

Many analysts try to estimate a P/E ratio for each stock by examining the historical relation between the stock and the P/E ratio of the market or some peer group such as industry. These P/E ratio comparisons are typically called *relative P/E ratios*. Investors must examine the P/E ratio of a specific industry relative to the Standard & Poor's Index, then take a look at the company relative to its *specific* industry segment. The *Standard & Poor's 500 Composite Stock Price Index* is broken down into dozens of industry *subindices,* each one having its own P/E ratio.

Several factors affect the relative P/E ratio. It is not in question that P/E ratios should be *higher* for industries that are expected to have rapid earnings growth. Here's an example.

EXAMPLE

Company A is currently earning *$1 per share*. Its earnings can be expected to grow 20 percent per year over the next 5 years. Company B *also* has current earnings of *$1 per share* and is expected to experience *10 percent* growth per year over the same 5-year interval. Company A will have earnings per share of $2.49 at the end of year 5, while company B will have earnings per share of $1.61. Would you expect both companies to sell at the *same* P/E ratio today (in year 1) if both companies have the same underlying risk?

No, of course not. All else equal company A would sell today at a higher price than company B because investors will have access to more earnings.

Note, however, this simple example makes some very important assumptions. First, both companies are assumed to have the same risk. If company A has more risk than company B, it is possible for both companies to sell at the same price or even (if the risk differential is very large) company B could sell at a higher price than company A. Second, we implicitly assume that expected earnings in years 5 through the entire life of the firm (which may be forever) are equal. If earnings of company B are expected to be much larger than earnings of company A, it is possible that company B will have a higher price than company A. Third, we assume that the earnings of both firms are comparable. Recall from the previous chapters on financial statements that firms can use different accounting methods on which to base financial statements. If firms use different accounting methods, then the earnings may not be comparable across firms.

Clearly it is important to understand that, *all else equal,* P/E ratios are larger for firms with high growth. All else equal, however, means that the firms must have the same risk, the earnings must be comparable, and the growth differential must be maintained for the entire life of the firms.

Growth cannot be valued blindly . . . Company A's growth may be the result of greater unit sales growth, more rapid selling price growth, or a leveraged capital structure. The growth could also be attributed to a favorable income tax status or even to an ultra-liberal set of accounting practices. The marketplace must take into analysis not merely the amount and certainty of earnings, but also the *sources* of earnings growth as well. The liquidity of the trading market from stock to stock could also affect P/E ratios. Other factors that could influence the P/E ratio could very well be the *charisma* of one company's management compared to the other's.

Several sophisticated mathematical models have been developed to predict relative P/E ratios. Using a technique known as *multiple regression analysis,* researchers can assign mathematical variables to each of the candidate factors that influence the ratios. By relating these variables to a *single estimator,* let's say a debt/assets ratio, a computerized model will estimate the contributory factor of each component as it relates to the *total* debt/assets ratio. Comparison of 100 companies over a 10-year period would yield regression statistics that could identify *significant* contributory factors. Is this complicated? Yes. Is it accurate? Sometimes. Although regression equations can be helpful in quantifying the impact of certain basic financial factors on the *normal P/E* ratios, they are not helpful in tracing influences of short-term P/E fluctuations.

Asset Values

Asset values or *asset transfer* values attempt to measure the value of corporations from the standpoint of the person in business. These valuations are concerned with the actual value of the business rather than the value of an equity as a partial share of reported earnings. As we have discussed, many corporate assets are *hidden* on the balance sheet. They could be part of LIFO reserves, for example. Other means of hiding assets include real estate ownership, assignable long-term leases, trade names, and overfunded pension liabilities. In such cases, the *narrow focus on earning power* can seriously underestimate the *value* of the corporation. Properly managed assets can and should produce a *stream* of earnings and dividends. Analysts who concentrate their focus on assets may be able to get a more accurate picture of growth potential and yield over time than those who are only concerned with historical and projected trends in corporate earnings.

Price/Sales Ratios

By dividing the most recent 12 months' revenues per share into the stock price, analysts can get the price/sales (P/S) ratio (which ranges from 0.4 to 0.8 for most of the larger companies). Ratios that exceed 0.8 usually indicate that the stock is overpriced, whereas those below 0.4 show the companies may have dangerously high debt levels, and additional investigation of the financial position is warranted. If the company is not going for a Chapter 11 (bankruptcy), low P/S ratios could also indicate good candidates for purchase of stock. Major exceptions to this would be companies that are in *high turnover businesses* with *low profit margins per dollar of sales* (e.g., supermarkets). Emerging growth companies can have P/S ratios in excess of 2.0 without being considered overpriced on their stock quotations. A warning, however: Ratios above 3.0 by this method are probably too high. The P/S ratio is particularly useful in companies that have extremely volatile earnings. Since there is no standardized method for normalizing the P/E ratio under these circumstances, the P/S ratio provides a convenient alternative to subjective analysis.

Let's review.

QUESTIONS

Place a "T" in front of the statements that are true and an "F" in front of those that are false.

_____ Net liquidation values can be obtained easily and reliably from a quick look at the balance sheet.

_____ Discounting dividends at the required rate of return reflects (to some extent) the actual degree of uncertainty about the overall accuracy of the estimates.

_____ We would expect a P/E ratio to range from 10 to 14 during times when investors look to the future with confidence.

_____ P/E ratios *should* be higher for industries that expect to experience rapid earnings growth.

_____ Multiple regression analyses are an easy way to find short-term P/E fluctuations.

_____ Overfunded pension liabilities should *not* be a focus in estimating the *value* of a corporation.

_____ A P/S ratio of 3.1 could indicate a good buy in an emerging high growth company.

ANSWERS

F   F
T   F
F   F
T

6
Fundamental Analysis

To understand the basic principles of securities analysis, the investor must first understand the distinction between the two main schools of thought that dominate this field—fundamental and technical analysis. *Fundamental analysis* looks to the economic indicators of performance for a company: its earnings, sales, assets, liabilities, cash flow, rate of return on equity, and the broad movement of economic activity often referred to as the business cycle. Fundamental securities analysts believe that these factors are important in deciding whether a particular stock represents a buy, sell, or hold position. The ability to anticipate changes in business conditions can be very helpful when determining the correct time to buy and/or sell securities. Most professional securities analysts place differing amounts of emphasis on particular ratios and factors.

In this chapter, we'll acquaint you with some of the methods of analyzing business, industry, and company cycles and how they affect stock prices. You'll also learn about certain characteristics to look for when analyzing a company you are interested in.

When analyzing a company, many fundamental analysts consult the brokerage firm's technical analysts to learn their feelings about a particular stock's trading pattern and price prognosis. Fundamental analysis is generally used to discover an appropriate stock whereas technical analysis is used to determine the right *time* to invest in that stock. Technical analysis will be discussed in the following chapter.

Typically, fundamental analysts start by taking a comprehensive view of the economy, move on to appraise an individual industry, and only at the final stage become concerned with the evaluation of a particular company and its stock. Essentially number crunchers, fundamental analysts rely heavily on ratio analysis and other numerical techniques to arrive at the true worth of a company's stock. As we mentioned before, they place emphasis on the trend in a company's assets, sales, and earnings, as reflected in the various ratios discussed in Chapter 4. These same ratios aid the fundamental analyst in developing questions to gauge the quality of a company's management and its direction.

The fundamental analyst looks to the future performance of a company over a period of at least 6 months and is not as concerned with the day-to-day price fluctuations of a company's stock.

Business Cycles and Stock Prices

In order to foresee major turning points in the general level of stock prices, the analyst attempts to forecast business cycle turning points several months in advance. Based on market observation, stock prices tend to decrease before the economy takes a downturn. Therefore, the natural assumption is that economic growth lies ahead of a recession—but not without a time delay. The market usually peaks approximately a few months (two to eight) before the economy takes a downturn.

It is worth mentioning that stock price highs and lows have usually occurred before turning points of general business activity. Many investors and analysts alike are often surprised when stock prices rise during relatively quiet business news and fall during a prosperous phase. This is to be expected because this is how the stock market behaves.

Some of the explanations for the behavior of the stock market are a little easier to understand than others. One theory is that investors in general have good foresight. They make investments based on what they think will happen to upcoming business activity rather than on what is currently happening. Another theory is a slight reversal of the former. It postulates that investors act on current developments, such as profit margins and corporate profits, rather than future developments. What happens as a result, according to this theory, is that investors who are profit oriented bid stock prices up and drive them down in anticipation of general business activity.

Yet a third theory maintains that stock price reversals lead to economic reversals by upsetting consumer confidence in spending decisions.

General Measurement of Market Price Movements

Although reports in the media go on about the rising and falling of the stock market on any given day, few people are aware of how market indices are constructed and what changes in these indices really mean. What is the significance of these indices? What do day-to-day changes in these indices signify?

Most investors believe that individual stocks move with the market as a whole—perhaps their individual portfolios increased in value as the overall market rose. Stock market indices meet a basic need of the investing public; that is, the need for a composite report on market performance. Market indices provide just such an indication of collective market movements to help the investor follow general business cycles.

Dow Jones Industrial Averages

The Dow Jones Industrial Average (DJIA) is the oldest and most popular market indicator series. This index is derived in two steps: First, the current prices of 30 large, well-known industrial stocks, which are listed on the New York Stock Exchange, are totaled. Then, this number is divided by a number that accounts for changes in the stocks comprising the index, as well as for stock splits.

Several criticisms however, have been directed at the accuracy and reliability of the DJIA. The objection is that the sample used for the series is too small and, by definition, limited to the most important companies in their respective industries. Perhaps the most significant criticism is that the DJIA is a price-weighted series. As such, a small percentage change in a high-priced stock in the series has an excessive effect on the overall index. Further, because the DJIA adjusts for stock splits, it is thought to be biased against stocks with high growth rates. Such stocks tend to split more often than others and hence lose weight in the series. Nevertheless, a fairly close relationship has been found between the daily changes in the DJIA and the other stock market indices used by analysts and investors.

Standard & Poor's Index of 500 Stocks

As an alternative to the price-weighted approach of the DJIA, Standard & Poor's Corporation was the first to develop a value-weighted index for measuring overall market performance. In this kind of index, the initial total market value of all stocks in the series is determined by multiplying the number of shares outstanding by the current market price. This initial market value then becomes the base for the series and is assigned an index value of 100. Market value is calculated on a daily basis and compared to the base market value, with any change reflected as a percentage variation from the market base. To overcome the criticism that the DJIA sample is too selective, Standard & Poor's included 500 stocks listed on the American Stock Exchange, as well as over-the-counter securities. However, while the 500 stocks in the Standard & Poor's Composite Index represent approximately 70 percent of the market value of all stocks on the exchange, they represent only about 28 percent of all exchange listings.

Other Listings: NYSE, AMEX, and NASD Indexes

The New York Stock Exchange (NYSE) has derived industrial, utility, transportation, and composite market value indices, with data back to 1940. Market prices as of December 31, 1965, were selected as the base and assigned a value of 50. Because the NYSE series includes all stocks listed on the exchange, there can be no criticism that the sample is too small. Because this is a value-weighted index, the issues of major companies still dominate major movements in this index.

Following in the footsteps of the New York Stock Exchange, the American Stock Exchange (AMEX) and the National Association of Securities Dealers (NASD) developed value-weighted indices to track movements in the AMEX and over-the-counter (OTC) markets combined.

Does a price-weighted or a value-weighted series give a more accurate picture of total market movements? Studies have shown that, over both the short and long run the difference between the price-weighted and value-weighted approaches is not as significant as the difference stemming from the stocks used to make up the sample, that is, NYSE, AMEX, or OTC stocks.

The Industrial Life Cycle

Making judgments about stock value is often easier and more accurate when the market as a whole is analyzed first; then the specific industry as it relates to the overall market is examined, and finally, the individual company in relation to that industry is studied.

Judging the value of a stock is strongly based on the corporation's sales and earnings, which are directly connected with the activity of the industry and the overall economy. Therefore we will take a look first at how to analyze the trends and cycles of industry sales and earnings and later at company performance.

The industrial life cycle is considered to be a useful framework for analyzing industry trends. Most product lines, and sometimes even marketing strategies, go through various stages of development. In the beginning, the company grows at a rapid rate. After the growth rate slows a bit, expansion continues but at a more moderate pace. Eventually, growth stops, and the company either remains stable or weakens and dies. When examining a company, you should always look at its beginnings, evaluate each surge of new activity or growth spurt, and appraise the profits or losses from those activities.

The Basic Model

The industrial life cycle is noted for occurring in four primary stages. The first, or initial growth, stage is often accompanied by a high rate of growth leading to highly profitable opportunities. Competition is fierce and many fledgling companies succumb to bankruptcy.

The second stage is often referred to as the rapid expansion stage, where after several years of proving themselves through internal expansion and consolidation, a few companies dominate an industry's overall business volume. They improve the quality and reduce the price of a product and broaden the market. Growth is still occurring at a rapid pace, but the company is more secure in that growth.

The third stage, labeled mature growth, shows the growth slowing down ever-so-slightly, but slowing nevertheless. As one industry grows older, newer products or services appear as the new blood grabs for a handle or a niche in the market. Because the market is reaching its saturation point, little can really be done to broaden that market with additional improvements or price cuts.

The last stage of growth actually constitutes three possibilities: (1) the industry may continue with very slow growth, (2) it may maintain its current growth level, or (3) its growth rate may decline to a point where its existence could be in jeopardy. If this last possibility becomes the scenario, the companies involved in this industry must concentrate on improving their productivity by becoming better at what they do, not necessarily by becoming bigger.

Let's review.

QUESTIONS

Are the following statements true or false?

1. The most rapid growth during the industrial life cycle occurs in the third stage.

2. The analysis of a company should begin with the developmental stages of each major activity in which the company engages.

ANSWERS

1. The statement is false. The first, or initial growth, stage is often accompanied by a high rate of growth leading to highly profitable opportunities.

2. The statement is true. When examining a company, you should always look at its beginnings, evaluate each surge of new activity or growth spurt, and appraise the profits or losses from those activities.

End-User Markets

To help determine if an industry is progressing on to the next stage of its life cycle, the markets for the industry's products must be evaluated. The market is identified by many factors, which can be geographic, consumer income bracket, consumer life-style, and the industry consuming the product. For example, the end-user markets for the semiconductor industry are telecommunications and office automation.

The growth rate in an industry can be kept active if the industry maintains the ability to compete with new product lines in both rapidly and adequately growing markets and if the industry *increases* its market share in its existing markets. On the contrary, if influence in a user market declines, the industry's growth will also decline.

Prices

So far, we've talked about how the ability to foresee business cycle turning points can help determine the turning points in the stock market as a whole. But how does this ability affect the overall trend of stock prices and the selection of a particular stock?

Price changes of stocks reflect many factors including some we've already mentioned: company sales and earnings. Other factors include the overpricing or underpricing of different stocks and their effect on the turning point of the general market. Accurate forecasts of the economy as a whole can and often do improve forecasts of changes in the success of different industries. However, forecasts of stock price changes in different industries need improvement.

Life Cycle of Prices

The concept of the industrial life cycle has been most useful in the analysis of sales volume. Overall profit margins and earnings patterns correspond to the stages of an industry that we discussed in the previous paragraphs.

Some of the more influential characteristics of the profit life cycle are as follows:

1. Revenues rise sharply for a time, rise more slowly, then finally level off.
2. The profit margin is in the negative column until revenues reach a critical point. Then margins, along with growing revenues, rise rapidly, which causes the level of earnings to rise as well.
3. Profit margins begin to level off after the mature growth stage.
4. Even though profit margins gradually slow down during the mature growth stage, earnings still continue to rise. This occurs because growth in revenue offsets the declining margins.

5. Earnings stabilize when revenue and profit margin trends offset each other. Sometimes earnings actually go down if declining revenues and profit margins have an overwhelming effect.

Analyzing the Company

As we discussed in Chapter 4, a *balance sheet* presents a company's condition at a specific point in time, usually the final business day of a quarter or a year. On one side of the balance sheet are the company's *assets;* that is, the company's funds or other things of value, listed in their order of liquidity. First come liquid assets, such as cash and cash equivalents, followed by increasingly illiquid assets, such as plant and equipment, which cannot be readily converted to cash.

The other side of the balance sheet presents the company's liabilities and net worth. *Liabilities,* which represent funds that the company owes, are presented in the order in which they come due. *Net worth,* or funds in excess of the funds owed, is equal to the difference between assets and liabilities. Expressed another way, a company's net worth represents what investors have put into the company plus earnings that have been retained in the company rather than paid out as dividends.

The two sides of a balance sheet—assets versus liabilities and net worth—must always be equal. Even when a company is insolvent (liabilities exceed assets), the two sides are kept equal by showing a negative net worth or deficit. The balance sheet therefore presents a static position of a company's accounts.

The *income statement* reflects a company's dynamics, by disclosing the results of a company's operations over a period, such as the 12 months reflected in an annual report or 3 months in a quarterly report.

Certain key elements in an income statement are of particular significance to securities analysts. Of primary importance are three areas:

1. *Sales* are the life blood of an operating company. A company cannot exist without a demand for its product.
2. *Operating income* is what a company has left after the cost of goods sold, depreciation, and selling, general, and administrative expenses.

3. *Net after-tax income,* commonly referred to as the "bottom line," is the income left after deducting interest expense, unusual income or expenses, and income taxes from the net operating profit. It is of particular significance to securities analysts because it represents the money the company has available either to pay dividends to the shareholders or to retain in the business for funding future growth.

Depreciation, which is one of the largest expenses for most companies, can significantly affect a corporation's cash flow. *Depreciation* is the allocation over time of the cost of replacing plant and equipment as they wear out or become obsolete. This expense is simply a bookkeeping entry that reflects no actual outflow of funds. For accounting purposes, therefore, cash flow from operations is assumed to equal net income plus depreciation (an expense). So, although *cash flow* is defined as the net difference between the money a company takes in and the money it pays out, depreciation is an expense that is added to the money taken in—not to the money paid out.

So then, how do securities analysts regard a company's balance sheet and income statement? If they feel that the true worth of the company's assets is not reflected in the stock's market price, they concentrate on the balance sheet and any changes in it. If the company's strength seems to lie in the growth of its sales and bottom line, they focus on the income statement.

In either instance, analysts study the trends in balance sheet and income statement ratios rather than in the absolute numbers. Their aim is to determine whether the company is expanding and growing or faltering and declining. A number of significant ratios are described in the following paragraphs.

Ratios: The Tools of Analysis

Ratio analysis enables analysts to deal with the numerical data in a company's balance sheet and income statement. They can compare the assets and performance of one company with those of other companies in the same industry, with companies in other industries, and with the economy as a whole.

Using liquidity ratios, securities analysts seek to answer such questions as the following:

Is the company capable of meeting its current obligations?

Does it have the liquidity (working capital) to continue to operate and grow?

What are the current assets available to meet current obligations?

Analysts use capital structure ratios to answer such questions as the following:

What is the nature of the company's capital structure?

Is the company too heavily in debt?

Does it rely on equity financing too much or does it have too many shares outstanding?

With payout ratios, analysts seek answers to such questions as the following:

How much of the company's earnings are paid out in dividends?

How much are retained in the business?

Liquidity Ratios

Liquidity ratios indicate the company's ability to repay debt, finance capital expenditures, and make other types of cash outlays.

The *current ratio* is equal to current assets divided by current liabilities. Current assets are assets that can be converted into cash within 1 year or less; current liabilities are obligations that typically must be paid off within 1 year.

A company's current ratio, which is essentially a measure of liquidity, is usually compared to the same corporation's past ratios as well as to those of other companies in the same industry. For most companies, a 2:1 current ratio is the norm. A ratio of 5:1 or more may suggest that the company has too much liquidity—that it is inefficiently run, not making aggressive use of its assets, and leaving itself vulnerable to a takeover.

Although financial leverage ratios are not liquidity ratios, they do provide an indication of the cash flow demands on a firm from debt. If the proportion of common stock to total capitalization is low, the volatility of earnings to common stock increases. Also, the ability of a company to meet its debt obligations has to be questioned. Thus, these ratios give analysts insight into a corporation's risk of bankruptcy.

For example, a combined bond and preferred stock ratio over 33 percent (the norm) may mark a company as having a high risk of bankruptcy and therefore as being very speculative. The exceptions are rail and utility companies, whose ratios may be quite high.

Some liquidity ratio formulas follow:

$$\text{Current ratio} = \frac{\text{Current assets}}{\text{Current liabilities}}$$

$$\text{Quick ratio} = \frac{\text{Current assets inventory}}{\text{Current liabilities}}$$

Capital (Debt-to-Equity) Structure Ratio

A capital structure ratio describes the relationship of a company's capital structure to common stock, preferred stock, or bonds (funded debt). A corporation's capital structure, or capitalization, is equal to the sum of capital from these three sources:

$$\text{Capitalization} = \text{Funded debt} + \text{Stockholders' equity}$$

Price/Earnings Ratio

The most commonly used measure of market risk is the price/earnings ratio, which gauges the support given to the current market price by the annual earnings per share. The formula for calculating the price/earnings (P/E) ratio is

$$\text{P/E ratio} = \frac{\text{Current market price}}{\text{Annual earnings per share}}$$

QUESTION

A company's common stock is selling at $30 per share, and the company earns $3 per share. What is the P/E ratio?

ANSWER

The P/E ratio is 10 : 1.

$$\frac{\$30}{\$3} = 10 : 1$$

Keep two things in mind when determining the P/E ratio. First, investors generally regard a company's stock as a growth investment if earnings are projected to increase at a rate far above the norm. In such a case, the company's stock will sell at a high P/E ratio, say, 15 : 1. Second, the general level of P/E ratios tracks the bullish or bearish sentiment in the marketplace. As people and institutions buy common stock more aggressively, the P/E ratios for individual stocks tend to increase.

QUESTION

Are low P/E stocks better investments than high P/E stocks?

ANSWER

Studies have shown that low P/E stocks perform better in the marketplace. Some risk is attached to high P/E stocks because any slowdown in the company's rate of growth may result in substantial selling off by institutions, who tend to have sizable holdings of high P/E stocks. The argument is also sometimes made that a high P/E tends to discount a lot of the company's future growth.

Current Yield

Yield is important to investors, typically retired persons and others living on fixed incomes, who seek current income from their investments as opposed to future income in the form of capital gain.

When talking about yield on stock, you are talking about the dividend yield and dividend payout ratios. The dividend yield ratio is equal to dividends divided by stock price. This ratio indicates the proportion of the rate of return on the stock that is derived from dividends.

The dividend payout ratio is a measurement of a company's percentage distribution to the common stockholders of net earnings after interest and taxes. The formula is

$$\frac{\text{Dividend}}{\text{payout}} = \frac{\text{Annual dividend paid to common shares}}{\text{After-tax earnings}} - \frac{\text{Preferred}}{\text{dividends}}$$

For example, if the annual dividend paid is $2 per share, earnings after taxes are $4 per share, and the company has no preferred stock outstanding (hence no preferred dividends):

$$\frac{\text{Dividend}}{\text{payout ratio}} = \frac{2}{4} = .50 \text{ or } 50\%$$

The norm is about 45 percent, the average dividend payout ratio for the Standard & Poor's 500 Index. The exceptions are utilities companies, which may average 80 percent or more.

The dividend payout ratio is an effective tool in determining whether a company's stock should be looked at as a growth or income situation. A growth company can earn more for its shareholders by retaining its earnings in the business and using the internally generated funds to finance capital expansion than by paying out dividends to its shareholders. As a result, growth companies typically retain a large portion of their earnings in the business and have an extremely low or nonexistent dividend payout ratio.

Although ratio analysis is a key tool of securities analysis, it is only as effective as the judgmental skill of the analysts using it. The ability to determine which ratios are significant in a particular situation comes only with time and experience.

Company Growth

Several factors are worth looking at when determining a company's overall growth. The analyst must determine the stage of the life cycle at which the industry is currently placed. This was mentioned earlier, but warrants repeating here because of its importance. Since many companies have diversified their operations over the years and perhaps have spread their worth among several industries, the life cycle segment of each of these industries must be individually determined and evaluated. For the most part though, the primary industry need only be examined. Major oil companies, auto manufacturers, retailers, and utilities are some of the companies that have the bulk of their operations in one industry.

Once a company's overall growth, prospective growth, and cyclical history have been examined in relation to the industry, the analyst can then look at the company's earnings sources. A company's earnings per share are a measure of the company's dollar return on its stockholders' equity. This dollar return can be divided by the per-share value of the stockholders' equity to calculate a rate of return on shareholders' equity.

The amount of earnings growth and dividend growth is determined by the company's dividend policy and its return on equity.

The other major source of growth in earnings per share is the company's book value per share. For many firms, this results from earnings retention. As we mentioned before, the amount of earnings retained is dependent upon shareholder dividends as well as projected use of those funds available.

QUESTION

A company's earnings per share are equal to its rate of return on stockholders' equity divided by the per-share value of the stockholders' equity. True or false?

> **ANSWER**
>
> The statement is false. A company's earnings per share are equal to the company's dollar return on its stockholders' equity. This can then be divided by the per-share value of the stockholders' equity to calculate a rate of return on equity.

Risks

Earnings-per-share relationships and book value per share are good indicators of investment opportunities. Sometimes they lead to special situations. Special situations have three major characteristics:

1. A corporate development occurs that makes the securities of the company attractive without consideration of the general economic, industry, or securities market conditions.
2. This particular development is fleeting in nature. If the opportunity is not seized at the peak of its specialness, the opportunity could be lost forever. The stock will still be valuable, but not as a special situation.
3. The gains or losses in the investment are easily estimated. The measure may not be precise, but the magnitude of potential gain or loss can be assessed.

The following types of corporate development generally lead to special situations:

Tender offer. A formal proposition to stockholders to sell their shares in response to a large purchase bid. The buyer customarily agrees to assume all costs and reserves the right to accept all, none, or a specific number of shares presented for acceptance.

Merger. The nonhostile and voluntary union of two corporations.

Liquidation. The voluntary or involuntary closing out of security positions. Proceeds of the company's assets are distributed to its shareholders.

Spin-off.   A distribution of stock in a company that is owned by another corporation and that is being allocated to the holders of the latter institution.

Management buyout.   An offer by management to purchase the firm at a premium over its present market price.

Management changes.   Firms experience management changes when the firm is performing poorly, a senior manager retires, or a group of major shareholders takes control of the board of directors.

Regulation.   Major changes in regulation such as the increase in automobile emission control regulations can have an impact on the firm.

Lawsuits.   Lawsuits for antitrust, legal liability, and so forth can have an impact on the future of the firm.

Management

The quality of management should be considered as a factor in a stock's evaluation, but not as the sole factor. Management's actions are reflected in the sales growth, in the rate of return on assets and on equity, and in the strength of the company's balance sheet. Decisions made by management today are reflected in tomorrow's numbers.

To help determine if the current management is not doing a worthwhile or even adequate job, some signs to look for include the following:

1. Watch for a repetitive product line over a long period of time. If nothing new is being introduced or attempted, then management may be out of touch with what the market wants and needs.
2. If executives are repeatedly hired by outside agencies instead of from the company's own management ranks, competent and talented people from within the company are possibly being overlooked.
3. Lawsuits against the company charging environmental pollution or discrimination. If social responsibility is being sidestepped, customers' and employees' needs may be also.
4. Low research and development (R&D) expenditures compared with the competition's R&D costs.

7

Technical Analysis

Fundamental analysis focuses on the basic economic factors underlying price movements. This approach is therefore said to study the *causes* of price movements. By contrast, technical analysis studies the *effects* of supply and demand—that is, the price movements themselves. In fact, technical analysis is also called *charting* because it is essentially the charting of actual price changes as they occur. The charting approach reflects the basic assumption of the technician that all influences on market action—from natural catastrophes to trading psychology—are automatically accounted for, or *discounted,* in price activity.

Given this premise, charting can be used for at least three purposes:

1. *Price forecasting.* The technician can project price movements either in tandem with a fundamental approach or solely on the basis of charted movements.
2. *Market timing.* Chart analysis is much better suited than the fundamental approach for determining exactly when to buy and sell.
3. *Leading indicator.* If market action discounts all influences on it, then price movement may be considered as a leading indicator and may be used in two ways. First, the chartist may—without regard for why prices are moving in one direc-

tion or the other—buy or sell. Second, an unusual price movement can be taken as a signal that some influence or another
on the market has not been accounted for in the fundamentalist's analysis or previous technical analysis and that further
study is required.

Technical analysis is also a popular method of forecasting price
movements of securities. Most followers use charts that record price
changes in various ways over a period of time. The methods used by
analysts differ slightly, but they all subscribe to the theory that
previous movements, properly interpreted, can indicate future patterns.

One point regarding technical analysis is important for all investors: If enough people *feel* that XYZ common stock is a good buy
at $27 per share, it *will become* a good buy if that level is reached.
The orders to purchase will cause a rise in the value of the stock
independent of any basic changes in the fortunes of the company.
Technical analysts are concerned with price, volume, timing, and
trend. Technicians give little consideration to those factors that are
signposts to the fundamentalist. According to the technicians, earnings, dividends, and new product development can all be "read" in
the price pattern. Most technical analysts believe that necessary
research can be gleaned from an interpretation of chart patterns.
Their basic belief is that what has happened in the past can forecast
what will happen in the future. Compare the chartist to a doctor who
specializes in cardiology: The doctor graphs the changing behavior of
the heart and from it can tell what has happened. From the information in the graph, the doctor notes problems that have existed and
concludes that they may well recur. Thus the doctor determines
strength or weakness from past performance and then judges future
prospects on that basis.

The chartist too believes in trends. Security prices tend to move in
one direction for a long period of time. Interruptions will occur, but
an interruption is not a reversal; it may provide an outstanding
opportunity for profit. Charts are best used for discovering short-
term potential. They are used to select levels that may indicate an
upward or downward movement, as opposed to the Dow theory
(which will be discussed later), which concerns itself with long-term
movements.

A complete study of technical analysis cannot be attempted here,
but a brief look at some of its more indicative characteristics and

patterns will provide an introduction to this market-timing device and also will serve as a companion piece to the synopsis of fundamental analysis we provided in the previous chapter.

Breadth of Market

One of the most popular techniques used to study major turning points of the market as a whole is breadth of market analysis. It is based on ideas concerning stock market cycles. Bull (favorable) markets are seen as extended affairs where individual stocks reach peaks gradually, with individual peaks progressing as the market averages rise toward a turning point. Bear (unfavorable) markets, on the other hand, are seen as dense collapses of many stocks in a short period of time. To find a condition of internal market weakness, technical analysts must determine whether many stocks are falling while the averages rise. Likewise, to find the nearing end of a bear market, technical analysts consider how extensive the selling pressure is. The scattering of a price rise or decline, in general, is called breadth of market.

Volume of Trading

In 1901, Charles Dow, an editor of *The Wall Street Journal,* wrote "Great activity means great movement whenever the normal balance between buyers and sellers is violently disturbed." Ever since then, technicians have gained perspective on the general health and trends of the market by following volume data.

There are several ways in which to follow volume trends, and analysts are constantly finding new ways to do so. However, the fundamental rule is really quite simple: Price follows volume.

Many volume-oriented technical analysts agree on the following principles regarding trading volume:

1. Expanding volume coupled with rising prices is a normal trait and has little to do with any prospective trend reversal.
2. A rally that attains a new price high with expanding volume indicates a potential trend reversal. The overall activity level is still considered lower than the previous rally, however.

3. If both price and volume expand slowly and then decline sharply, a trend reversal will result.
4. After a market rise of several months, a subsequent weak price rise with high volume indicates a bearish situation. Conversely, after a decline, little price change and heavy volume indicate a bullish situation.
5. A selling climax usually occurs when prices fall quickly for an extended length of time, and volume is expanding. As a result, prices are expected to rise.

Test your understanding.

QUESTION

As a general rule, stock prices tend to follow volume. True or false?

ANSWER

The statement is true. Charles Dow said it himself, and since that time, technicians have followed volume data very closely to determine the volume trends and price action.

Supply/Demand Analysis

Supply/demand analysis is used to measure imbalances between new stock offerings and expected investment requirements for common stocks. If offerings are numerous in relation to the demand, stock prices will decrease. Likewise, if offerings are fewer and demand is greater, prices will increase.

New offerings relate to the expected needs of companies to finance spending plans by offering new equity, or shares of their company's stock. The more money they need, the greater number of stocks they will offer for sale to the public.

Demand factors constantly face dramatic changes. Depending on overall market trends, pension fund purchases of common stock, for example, either increase when share prices increase or decrease when the prices fall. When making a supply/demand forecast, analysts must take into account the predominant expectations of the market as a whole.

Let's review.

QUESTION

Which method of technical analysis measures imbalances between new stock offerings and anticipated demand for common stock?
1. Upside/downside analysis
2. Relative strength analysis
3. Supply/demand analysis
4. Breadth of market analysis

ANSWER

The correct answer is (3). If a company offers more shares of stock than the market really needs or wants, price per share will go down.

Contrary Opinion Theory

The general concept of contrary opinion is basically to "go against the crowd" regarding market attitudes. Going against the grain and believing in something totally opposite to popular opinion are not new to Wall Street. The popularity of this concept continually waxes and wanes and is currently experiencing a surge.

Through experience with this concept over the years, analysts have developed a number of tools and techniques to measure popular opinion regarding stock prices. They have also learned how to determine which opinion is in favor at any particular time, so they can take the opposite position in the market. Market sentiment is not always predictable, and the overall consensus regarding that sentiment is not always reliable. The majority may not be wrong in their feelings about market trends.

Odd-Lot Trading

The behavior of the small investor is a focal point of interest for many market forecasters. Some go so far as to say, "The odd-lot customer is always wrong." This is an overstatement, but consistent with the contrary opinion theory. Odd-lot traders frequently become heavy buyers as the market nears its top and reduce their buying in a down market prior to a rally. The changes in the odd-lot customer's buying can therefore be charted and used as an effective market signal.

Odd-lot purchases normally exceed sales. This results from the fact that clients often purchase an odd lot on a number of occasions until they accumulate a round lot. Therefore the subsequent sales will not be reflected in the daily odd-lot figures but will become part of the normal round-lot trading volume. Odd lots on the New York Stock Exchange are generally handled directly by the specialist. A customer wishing to purchase 50 shares of General Electric buys direct from the specialist, not from another client with a similar amount to sell. Thus total purchases and sales of odd lots directly reflect the attitude of small investors and can easily be studied for changing trends. Working from the normal imbalance of purchases versus sales, analysts watch the behavior pattern of the odd-lot purchaser. When it indicates a significant change of direction, an adherent to this type of trading makes a commitment—in the opposite direction.

Now try this question.

QUESTION

Which of the following is the underlying assumption of odd-lot trading analysis?

1. Small investors buy most heavily at market tops and sell most heavily at market bottoms.
2. Small investors tend to buy before market lows and sell before market highs.
3. Small investors buy most heavily at the bottom and sell most heavily at the top.
4. Current behavior of small investors is a clue to future behavior of large investors.

ANSWER

The correct answer is (1). Garfield A. Drew, who popularized the odd-lot theory, has noted that odd-lot customers frequently become heavy buyers as the market nears its top and reduce their buying in a down market just before a rally. The general theory is that the sophisticated investor should sell when the public increases its buying in relation to its selling and vice versa.

Short Selling

A short sale is the sale of a security that one does not own or does not intend to deliver (also known as a short against the box). The seller arranges to borrow the security and delivers the borrowed stock to the purchaser. The usual reason for a short sale is an anticipated decline in the market value of the security shorted. The seller hopes to repurchase it at a lower price and realize a profit.

The stock exchanges make a compilation of the short interest as of the fifteenth day of each month and report it to the media four business days later. At first glance, one would think that a sharp increase in short sales would presage a decline in the market. But the user of this technique thinks otherwise. Short sellers at some future point become buyers of stock to cover their positions. This cushion of potential buyers will support a declining market and may even accelerate a rising one. Short sellers may repurchase when the market goes up to limit their losses, and by doing so, they give impetus to the advance.

The short selling technique can be applied to the overall market or to particular issues. The conclusions are based on the size of the short position as related to average daily volume. If the short interest exceeds one day's average volume, the picture begins to look bullish. Should the short interest rise above $1\frac{1}{2}$ times the daily volume, analysts believe that the cushion is now large enough to indicate a buy signal. If enough adherents begin to purchase, the stock will rise. The short seller may then be forced to cover, and a further rise will result.

QUESTION

Analysts generally believe that a high short interest ratio is bearish and a low ratio is bullish. True or false?

ANSWER

The statement is false. If the short interest exceeds one day's average volume, the picture begins to look bullish. Should short interest rise above 1½ times the daily volume, the number of buyers is large enough to indicate a buy signal.

Mutual Fund Positions

One of the more reliable techniques of the contrary opinion theory is the analysis of changes in mutual fund cash positions. These positions are measured by the percentage of total mutual fund assets. These assets can be held either in cash or cash equivalents. The Investment Company Institute reports these figures on a monthly basis. Portfolio management opinion is generally considered, not the opinion of mutual fund holders. As a general rule, the greater the cash amount of the funds, the more favorable the market outlook. When uninvested funds are returned to the market, stock prices usually go up. Also, the lower the cash position, the less favorable the market looks.

Price Charts and Stock Selection Techniques

Dow Theory

The Dow theory is based on the early twentieth-century writings of Charles Dow. His ideas on the movements of stock prices were elaborated on by his colleague S. A. Nelson. Nelson named Dow's hypotheses the Dow theory.

Using the Dow Jones averages as its base, the theory proposes that these market averages rise or fall in *advance* of similar changes in business activity. By properly reading the averages, you get a prediction of things to come and can accurately plan investments based on prior price movements. Although it was never considered a get-rich-quick scheme by its originators, its adherents claim the theory is a reliable method of predicting future market direction.

The theory looks at three basic movements in the market, which are discussed here in order of importance.

Primary Movements

The *primary movement* is long term and may last from 1 to 5 years. This is the overall trend of the market and is the most important reading. You must be able to differentiate between brief reversals of the major trend and reversals from a bull to a bear market and vice versa.

Secondary Movements

Secondary movements reverse the primary movement and last for short periods, perhaps 1 to 3 months. As many as three to five of these shifts may occur during a bull or bear market before a trend reversal is indicated. The secondary movements provide information for medium-term trading decisions. More important, they help you to anticipate the life expectancy of the primary movement. Experienced analysts measure the percentage of variance from the primary movement, correlate it with the time it takes to reach that level, and, using historical precedent for that issue, project the duration potential of the primary movement.

Figure 7.1 shows a graph representing both primary and secondary movements. Note the primary movement illustrated between points *A* and *B* (upward) and then between points *B* and *F* (downward). The temporary, short-lived reactions between points *A* and *B* are secondary movements, as are the short rallies between points *B* and *F*. The Dow theorists believe that an upward trend is not reversed until one of those secondary reactions penetrates the bottom of a previous reaction, such as that which occurred at point *D* in relation to *C*. Conversely, the downward trend is reversed when a secondary movement rally penetrates the top of a previous rally, as happened when point *G* rose above *E*. Analogies are often drawn between primary and secondary movements and the seas. Primary

FIGURE 7.1   Dow Jones Primary and Secondary Movements

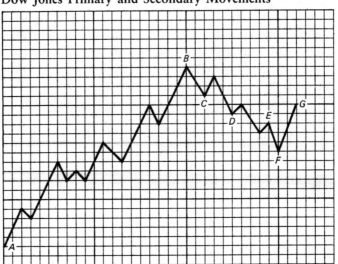

SOURCE   Pessin and Hyman, "Principles of Technical Analysis: Reading and
Understanding Financial News" in Volume 3: *The Securities Industry*.

movements are comparable to the incoming and ebb tides, whereas
secondary movements represent ocean waves influenced by those
flows.

Daily Fluctuations

Daily fluctuations are of little consequence to longer term market
movements. They are not indicative of primary or secondary movements and are often emotional reactions. They are like ripples that
appear on the waves of the sea, to use our earlier analogy. Pro-
ponents of the Dow theory hold that all factors concerning market
conditions are built into the averages. It is unnecessary therefore to
consider sales, earnings, dividends, production costs, or the hundreds
of other factors included in fundamental analysis. These elements are
implicit in the averages, and their effects can be clearly read.

Price Patterns

When price movements are charted, they describe a predictable pattern. Some price patterns indicate a trend reversal and are therefore
called *reversal patterns*. Others, called *continuation patterns*, reflect

pauses or temporary reverses in an existing trend and usually form more quickly than reversal patterns.

Some of the more basic patterns are described in the following paragraphs.

Reversal Patterns

Head and Shoulders

Perhaps the best known of reversal patterns, the head and shoulders has three clear peaks, with the middle peak (the head) higher than the ones before and after it (the shoulders). As you can see in Figure 7.2, the neckline is the trendline drawn to connect the two troughs between the peaks. A close below the neckline signals the completion of the pattern and an important market reversal. A breakaway gap (an area on the chart where no trading takes place) at the point of penetration through the neckline lends weight to the probability that a true reversal has taken place. The minimum extent of the reversal can be estimated. To do so, measure the distance from the head to the neckline and project the same distance from the breakthrough point in the neckline. A return move is likely, but it generally does not penetrate the neckline.

FIGURE 7.2   Head and Shoulders Pattern

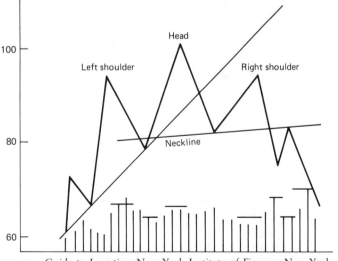

SOURCE   *Guide to Investing*, New York Institute of Finance, New York, 1987, p. 225.

Saucers

In an uptrend, this pattern may be referred to as an inverted saucer or rounding top. During a downtrend, it can be a rounding bottom or bowl. Regardless of its name, the pattern consists of a gradual turning of the trend on diminishing volume. Examples are shown in Figures 7.3 and 7.4.

No precise measurement can be made of the extent of the reversal by means of a saucer. The duration and size of the prior trend have some bearing on the new trend, as does the time the saucer takes to form.

Continuation Patterns

Continuation patterns represent pauses in the current trend, rather than reversals in the making.

FIGURE 7.3   Saucer Top

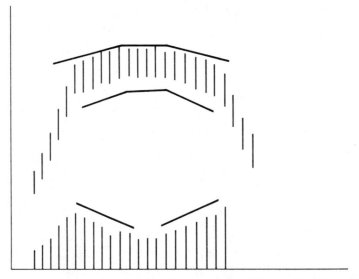

SOURCE   *Guide to Investing*, New York Institute of Finance, New York, 1987, p. 226.

FIGURE 7.4   Saucer Bottom

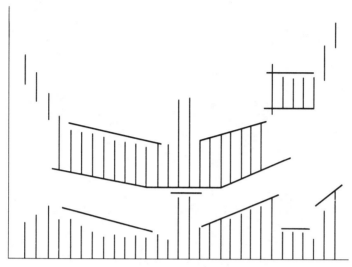

SOURCE *Guide to Investing*, New York Institute of Finance, New York, 1987, p. 227.

Symmetrical Triangle

Also known as the coil, the symmetrical triangle pattern forms, on diminishing volume, as a triangle that narrows evenly from left to right, with at least four reference points. This is illustrated in Figure 7.5. The trend may be expected to resume, with a closing price outside the triangle, sometime after one-half and three-quarters of the traingle's length is developed. Occasionally, there is a return move on light volume, but the penetrated trendline of the triangle acts as support in an uptrend or as resistance in a downtrend. In either direction, volume generally picks up as the trend resumes.

Rectangle

Also known as a trading range or congestion area, the rectangle pattern typically reflects a consolidation period before a resumption of the current trend. Refer to Figure 7.6.

In an uptrend, the volume is heavier on the rallies than on the setback, and a rectangle is probable. In a downtrend, a rectangle is likely if the dips are accompanied by heavier volume than the rallies.

FIGURE 7.5   **Triangle**

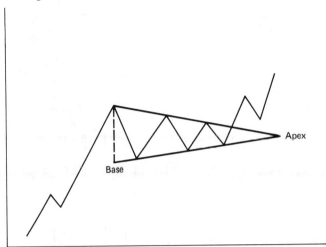

SOURCE   *Guide to Investing,* New York Institute of Finance, New York, 1987, p. 227.

Bar Charts

The technical analyst generally uses two working assumptions: (1) markets move in trends and (2) trends persist. The reasoning is that if market action discounts all influences, then prices move not randomly, but in trends. Identifying the trend at an early enough stage enables the trader to take the appropriate positions. One of the tools

FIGURE 7.6   **Upside Trend from a Sideways Market**

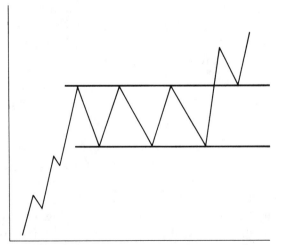

SOURCE   *Guide to Investing,* New York Institute of Finance, New York, 1987, p. 229.

used to track price movements and thus to identify trends is the bar chart.

Constructing a bar chart is simple. We've done one for you in Figure 7.7. At the top of the chart enter the name of the contract. To the vertical axis assign a price scale—days, weeks, or months. On a daily bar chart, every 5-day period (a trading week) is usually marked by a vertical line that is heavier than the others. For each day, the high, low, and closing (or settlement) prices are plotted. A vertical line, or bar, connects the high and low prices. A horizontal tick to the right of the bar indicates the closing price. (A tick on the left side of the bar marks the opening price for the day.)

Point and Figure (P&F) Charts

The other type of chart used by the technical analyst is the point and figure (P&F) chart, but unlike bar charts, P&F charts record only price movements; if no price change occurs, the chart remains the

FIGURE 7.7   Constructing a Bar Chart

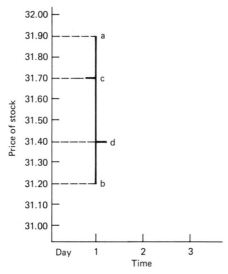

a: The high price for the day, $31.90
b: The low price for the day, $31.20
c: The opening price (not always on the bar chart), $31.70
d: The closing price, $31.40

SOURCE   *Guide to Investing*, New York Institute of Finance, New York, 1987, p. 215.

same. Volume is indicated only by the number of recorded price changes, not as a separate entity. Although traditionally ignored, gaps may be represented by empty boxes.

Point and figure charts have at least two major advantages over bar charts. First, they can be used on a intraday basis to identify support, resistance, and other price-related data that bar charts miss completely. Second, P&F charts are more flexible than bar charts in that the analyst can vary the size of the box and the reversal criterion, either of which can drastically change the appearance of the formation.

On a P&F chart, the analyst moves one row of boxes to the right each time the market reverses. The question you may be wondering about then, is what causes a reversal? Is a one-box change in direction a reversal, or is it three boxes worth of movement?

A P&F chart constructed with each box equal to one point and a three-box reversal criterion is a "1 × 3" chart. Figure 7.8 illustrates this. The analyst can make the same data plot differently—and make the chart less sensitive—by changing either the size of the box or the reversal criterion.

FIGURE 7.8   P&F Chart

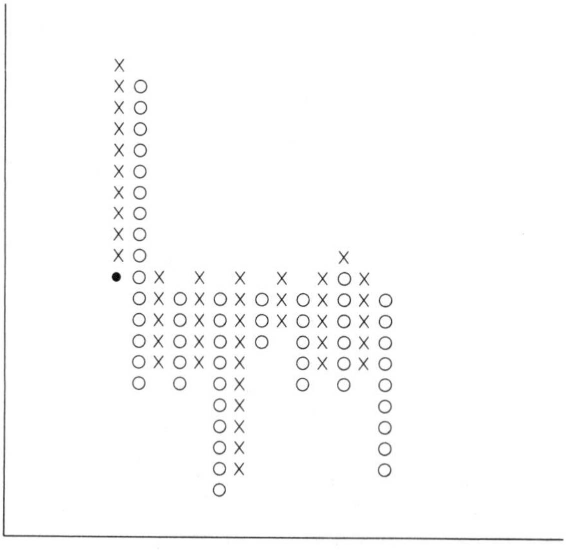

SOURCE   *Guide to Investing,* New York Institute of Finance, New York, 1987, p. 233.

Moving Average

As you may have surmised, the technical approach to investing can be a subjective practice, with two analysts in total disagreement over a pattern. Moving averages represent a step toward making a chart analysis more scientific.

A moving average is an average of closing prices over a certain number of days. For example, a 10-day moving average includes the past 10 days' prices. It is "moving" because as the latest day's prices are included in the average, the oldest day's prices are left out.

The moving average is also a trend-tracking tool. Typically represented on a chart as a curving line laid over the price movements, the moving average "smoothes out" the trend, enabling analysts to see whether prices are in or out of line. Thus, as a market follower, it signals whether a trend is still in effect or has reversed.

The responsiveness of a moving average to price movement depends on the number of days included in the calculation. Generally, the fewer the days included, the more closely the average tracks the price action. A 5- or 10-day average, for example, would "hug" the market activity more closely than one of 40 days.

Try this question.

QUESTION

A moving average is designed to reveal the underlying direction and rate of change of a highly volatile set of numbers. True or false?

ANSWER

The statement is true.

New analysts sometimes mistakenly regard technical analysis techniques as infallible—or nearly so. Their subliminal assumption is sometimes that, by drawing the trendlines associated with a pattern, they can "make" the projected price movement happen.

But perhaps the first rule in technical analysis is that there are no "rules" as such. A pattern will probably develop as anticipated, but it is not certain to do so. That is why chartists use the word "indicator," not "rule" and surely not "guarantee."

Analysts must combine all they know and all they see before taking a position. They must bring to bear the findings of their fundamental studies, their awareness of the market and industry in general, and their willingness to review indicators other than price constantly. Only then can they reasonably expect to profit from their trading.

Index